THE TRIUMPH OF GOD

The Essence of Paul's Thought

J. Christiaan Beker

translated by
Loren T. Stuckenbruck

Fortress Press   Minneapolis

THE TRIUMPH OF GOD
The Essence of Paul's Thought

Copyright © 1990 Augsburg Fortress.

First English-language edition published in 1990 by Fortress Press, Minneapolis. Original German edition published in 1988 under the title DER SIEG GOTTES copyright © Verlag Katholisches Bibelwerk GmbH.

Library of Congress Cataloging-in-Publication Data

Beker, Johan Christiaan, 1924–
    [Sieg Gottes. English]
    The triumph of God : the essence of Paul's thought / J. Christiaan
Beker : translated by Loren T. Stuckenbruck.
        p.   cm.
    Translation of: Der Sieg Gottes.
    Includes bibliographical references.
    ISBN 0-8006-2438-6 (alk. paper) : $8.95
    1. Bible.   N.T.   Epistles of Paul—Theology.   2. Paul, the
Apostle, Saint.   I. Title.
BS2651.B4513   1990
225.9'2—dc20   90-35463
                                                                     CIP

The paper used in this publication meets the minimum requirements of American National Standard for Information Sciences—Permanence of Paper for Printed Library Materials, ANSI Z329.48-1984.   ∞™

Manufactured in the U.S.A.   AF 1-2438

94   93   92   91   90   1   2   3   4   5   6   7   8   9   10

To the Memory of John A. Hollar,
faithful friend, imaginative theologian, and superb editor

Contents

Preface

The appearance of this book is due to the initiative of
two persons for which I am very grateful.

In 1986 Helmut Merklein, New Testament professor at
the Catholic Theological Faculty in Bonn (West Germany)
asked me to prepare an abridged version of my book *Paul
the Apostle: The Triumph of God in Life and Thought* (Fortress
Press, 1980) for the series Stuttgarter Bibel-Studien (SBS),
(Katholisches Bibelwerk, Stuttgart), of which Professor
Merklein is the co-editor.

The book appeared in 1988 with the title *Der Sieg Gottes:
Eine Untersuchung zur Struktur des paulinischen Denkens*
(SBS, 132).

Shortly after its appearance, my good friend and coun-
selor John A. Hollar, the late editorial director of Fortress
Press, encouraged me to translate the version, which I had
prepared in German, into English and to add my recent
article as a supplement, "Paul the Theologian: Major Motifs in Pauline Theology" (*Interpretation* 43, October 1989,
352–65).

I agreed with John Hollar's suggestion for two reasons.
First of all, it seemed useful to present to a wider readership
the basic results of my approach to Paul's thought, without
the need to consult the exegetical details of my voluminous

Paul the Apostle. Moreover, I decided to incorporate sec-
tions of my *Paul's Apocalyptic Gospel* (Fortress Press, 1982)
into the present volume, because the discussion of the
apocalyptic character of Paul's gospel exhibits more clarity
and simplicity in that book than in *Paul the Apostle* (see
chapter 2 below).

Second, my attempt to summarize my earlier work on
Paul's thought has an important corollary. It shows that
the controversy about Paul throughout the centuries continues in our own time, evident in the diversity of new
perspectives on his person and thought. It is superfluous,
therefore, to claim that my delineation of "the essence" of
Paul's thought is in any way finalized or fixed. With respect
to Paul—as with all other seminal figures in the history of
thought—we are always *in via,* "on the way," and must
continuously draw new insights from the community of
scholarship.

In the next few pages I will discuss briefly the extent to
which some of these new insights impinge on my own
construal of Paul's thought.

This book posits two pillars as the foundations of Paul's
thought: (1) the interaction between coherence and contingency in Paul's interpretation of the gospel and (2) the
apocalyptic character of his gospel.

1. The interaction between coherence and contingency
constitutes a peculiar dialectic in Paul's hermeneutical activity. Since Paul is not a systematic theologian, but rather
an interpreter of the gospel, the *method* of his interpretation
is a crucial issue. The special character of Paul's interpretation is marked by his ability to embody in his thought
and praxis the movement of the incarnation, that is, the
condescension of God into the depth of the human condition, so that the eternal Word of the gospel is able to
become ever anew a word on target for the people to whom
the gospel is addressed.

However, although Paul has a fundamental conviction
about the abiding "truth of the gospel" (Gal. 2:5, 14; cf.
Phil. 1:7, 27), so that the truth of the gospel is not com-
promised for the sake of opportunistic strategic victories,

the precise content and contours of his fundamental convictions—what I call "the coherence of the gospel"—cannot simply be ascertained and picked off by a surface reading of the Pauline text.

I suggest in my book that the special character of Paul's interpretation of the gospel manifests itself in the dialectical interaction between coherence and contingency (see pp. 3–9 and 15–19). In other words, the contingency of situations requires of Paul a specific adaptation of the gospel's coherence in order to allow the gospel to execute its proper function within the diverse circumstances of Paul's various audiences.

However, if Paul's interpretation is marked by such a "fusion of horizons" between coherence and contingency, my proposal needs to be corrected (see Appendix, pp. 118–22). The terminology of coherence and contingency is indeed useful in that it suggests that Paul's communication of the gospel is neither a doctrinal monologue that he imposes on his hearers nor an opportunistic structure that he shifts arbitrarily to accommodate his audiences. However, my terminology is misleading because it articulates in terms of distinct bifurcational concepts ("coherence" and "contingency" as distinctive concepts) what can only be grasped in symbolic terms. Conceptual analysis occurs at a level of abstraction and defines as distinct entities what in Paul's world of thinking must be integrated, not separated.

In other words, the nature of symbolic language and its function in Paul need to be more thoroughly investigated. The fusion of the coherent center with its contingent expression in Paul demonstrates that symbols overlap and interact with each other, so that a particular symbol that is relevant to one specific situation can be integrated with another symbol that speaks to a different situation.

In other words, my *conceptual* distinction between coherence and contingency oversimplifies and in some sense distorts the method of Paul's own interpretive thinking. To be sure, in some ways I was aware of the symbolic structure of Paul's thought, for example, in preferring the language of "coherence" over that of "core" (p. 61), in order to emphasize that Paul's fundamental convictions express themselves as a "network of interlocking parts" (pp. 61, 111) rather than as inflexible doctrinal concepts; moreover, a similar awareness made me emphasize "the basic fluidity" and "the fusion of horizons" between Paul's basic convictions and their interaction with contingent situations (p. 111; Appendix, pp. 121–22). However, these "pointers" require clearly a more fundamental inquiry into the basic nature of Paul's thought and language than I have provided.

2. The apocalyptic texture of the gospel constitutes the second pillar of Paul's interpretation of the gospel. "Far from considering the apocalyptic worldview a husk or a purely contingent symbol, it constitutes the master-symbol for the interpretation of the gospel" (Appendix, p. 124).

W. Wrede's comment in his book on Paul of 1904 became for me the fundamental key for unlocking Paul's thought: "The whole Pauline conception of salvation is characterized by suspense; a suspense which strains forward to the final release, the actual death. The earthly life is not the setting in which salvation becomes complete. He [Paul] believed with all his might in the speedy coming of Christ and the approaching end of the world. In consequence, the redemptive act of Christ, which lay in the past and the dawn of the future glory lay, in his view, close together. All references to the redemption as a completed transaction swing around at once into utterances about the future" (*Paul*, 105–6).

Paul's coherent center is marked not only by an apocalyptic matrix and pattern but also by a future orientation, which gives his thought its driving thrust. The pulsating quality of his thought does not find a respite until it climaxes in the arrival of the triumph of God which will turn all present approximations and ambiguities into the joy of everlasting peace.

My emphasis on Paul's christological apocalyptic involves a radical shift in traditional conceptions of Paul's theology (see p. 112). Stimulated by the studies of A. Schweitzer and E. Käsemann, I am recasting Paul's theology as a theocentric theology of hope rather than as a christocentric salvation-history (O. Cullmann) or as an existentialist theology of the cross (R. Bultmann). A theology of hope views the present as the dawn of the future and the future as the full actualization of the present.

This perspective opens up new hermeneutical possibilities for a present appropriation of Paul's thought and demonstrates how catalytic the Pauline text is for our reflection.

(a) Paul's theology of hope highlights the importance of his theocentric thinking because it does not culminate in the *Christ-event* as the consummation of history but in the actualization of *God's* sovereignty and triumph (cf. Rom. 5:1-10; 8:17-39; 1 Cor. 15:1-58).

Although it would be wrong to downplay christo-logy in favor of theo-logy, we must be aware of the integral connection between apocalyptic and theocentrism. Moreover, we must remember that throughout the history of interpretation, Paul's apocalyptic center has been dissipated by at least two events: (1) the rejection of the apocalyptic worldview and its subsequent interpretation as a removable husk, a foil for human self-understanding, or a form of realized eschatology; (2) a concomitant Christocentrism that, especially since Nicaea and Chalcedon, intended to protect the sovereignty and unity of God but actually fostered a type of Christomonism, particularly within the construal of an immanent Trinity. A full immanental Trinitarian hermeneutic seems to compel an interpretation of Paul's Christology in ontological rather than functional terms and thus fuses God and Christ to the detriment of the coming final glory of God, to which, according to Paul, Christ is subordinate and for which he lived and died.

(b) The theocentric aspect of Paul's thought has important consequences—not only for a Christian dialogue with Judaism and other non-Christian religions in our world, but especially for new construals of a biblical theology. It is a fact of modern times that books on "biblical theology" have practically vanished, whereas separate theologies of the Old or New Testament continue to flourish. Once the theocentric emphasis of the Old Testament is conjoined with similar emphases of New Testament authors like Paul, the importance both testaments assign to the category of hope, that is, the hope in a "new heaven and a new earth" (Isa. 65:17), where "all flesh will see the glory of the Lord" (Isa. 40:5), could become a keystone for a biblical theology.

(c) Moreover, Paul's apocalyptic theology challenges us to rethink our traditional conceptions of salvation and ethics. The center of Paul's thought is misunderstood when it is located in individual justification or in the equation of redemption with individual heavenly bliss or in a sectarian and elitist ecclesiology that defines itself simply *over against* the world.

The universal scope of God's coming reign necessitates a radical conception of the church *for* the world. Christians are only then "in Christ" when they become partners in God's cosmic redemptive plan for his world. "Since the human being is placed within the power structures of the world, there is a profound solidarity and interdependence" not only between all people in the world, but also between our "inner world," our "social world," and our "ecological world" (p. 27).

This solidarity under the lordship of sin and death manifests itself in the compulsive will to power of the absolute subject, which exercises its lust for domination not only in exploiting other people but also in destroying the delicate balance of nature.

Through God's action in Christ this solidarity of sin and death is replaced not by a world-neglecting individualism but by the solidarity of the "new creation." Therefore, Christians are called upon to embody their hope in God's coming triumph in "worldly" acts of solidarity and compassion, and in a responsible stewardship of God's world.

Moreover, the praxis of solidarity in acts of compassion and stewardship necessarily involves the Christian in another dimension of solidarity, a solidarity-in-suffering. Indeed, "we know that the whole creation has been groaning in travail together until now" (Rom. 8:22).

The cosmic powers that seem to rule our world—notwithstanding God's presence in Christ among us—cause not only innumerable instances of undeserved suffering but also many forms of inexplicable and meaningless suffering. Thus a solidarity-in-suffering manifests itself not only as a bold struggle against the sufferings of injustice but also as a silent presence of hope in the midst of the suffering of death. For, according to Paul's gospel, this solidarity-in-suffering may take place against a horizon of hope—the hope that the burden of suffering will be lifted from God's creation and be replaced by God's joyful presence at the time of his triumph.

The cosmic hope of the Christian, then, is able to resist not only all egoism and privatization of bliss, but also every form of denying, repressing, or spiritualizing the awesome reality of death in our world.

These comments indicate that my interest in Paul focuses not only on historical questions but also on the theological dimensions of his thought.

For instance, Paul's way of doing theology demonstrates that the interaction between the abiding word of the gospel and its contingent application involves every interpreter of the gospel in inescapable risks, not only because our perception of the situations to which the gospel is to be addressed may be erroneous but also because all of us are so easily tempted to distort the truth of the gospel for the sake of accommodating our hearers.

Moreover, we must understand that Paul's method of interpretation is inseparable from the apocalyptic coordinates of his gospel. Since a theocentric apocalyptic forms the matrix of the gospel and gives it its pulsating future thrust, we cannot but conclude that Paul's Christology stands in the service of the sovereignty of God, which culminates in his coming triumph over everything that resists his will.

The apocalyptic character of Paul's gospel, which operates in terms of cosmic power structures and focuses on a cosmic horizon, challenges us to rethink the importance of apocalyptic as an integral part of the gospel. For instance, is Paul's gospel able to address more adequately than other formulations of the gospel some of the urgent issues of our time? I have in mind the viability of a cosmic Christian hope, and the possibility of an ethic of solidarity that will encompass not only our ecological stewardship of God's creation but also our compassion for the oppressed in God's world.

Last, but not least, I want to thank my graduate student Loren T. Stuckenbruck for the difficult job of translating a condensed German version into readable English, Renee Fall, associate editor of Fortress Press, for her meticulous editorial work on the book, and my faculty secretary Joseph P. Herman for his care and expertise in producing a final manuscript.

PART ONE

THE PAULINE LETTER

1

The Hermeneutical
Problem

It has often been observed that the letters of Paul function as substitutes for his personal presence. In almost every letter, therefore, Paul includes information concerning his activities, his future plans and wishes, his intent to make a personal visit to the church in question, or his reasons why he has thus far been hindered from coming.

The Pauline letters are wholly concerned with and related to concrete situations. Since the work of Adolf Deissmann,[1] the "official epistle" has been distinguished from the "private letter," and Paul's writings have been customarily regarded as private correspondence. Although this characterization correctly assesses the occasional nature of Paul's letters, it deserves to be emphasized that Paul has not merely supplied his readers with casual, spontaneous remarks that relate to particular problems. Admittedly, his letters are concerned with specific occasions, but Paul treats these thoroughly (as in 1 Corinthians). The letters are indeed personal, but not simply private. They do not express a series of momentary impulses, but rather make authoritative claims. Even a polemical "fly sheet" such as Galatians reflects a carefully designed structure, as Hans Dieter Betz has shown.[2] Colossians—though it was not written

---

1. Deissmann, *Light from the Ancient East*.
2. Betz, "The Literary Composition and Function of Galatians."

by Paul himself, belonging instead to Pauline tradition—illustrates the semi-official character of Paul's letters: "When this letter has been read among you, have it read also in the church of the Laodiceans; and see that you read also the letter from Laodica" (Col. 4:16). Even a personal letter such as Philemon is sent to a house church (Philemon 2). Paul's writings were read during public worship services from the beginning (1 Thess. 5:27; cf. Eph. 3:4). Thus his letters are not just personal, occasional writings that only react to specific circumstances belonging to a definite time and place. Rather, they bear an authoritative character made clear by their official form, especially in the opening and closing formulations. They represent a unique phenomenon among the letters of Hellenistic and Roman authors. The formula "grace be with you and peace" (e.g., Rom. 1:7) is neither an addition to the normal Jewish letter nor a substitute for the customary "greeting" (*chairein*).

The official form of Paul's letters underscores his apostolic and authoritative claims. Their official structure, liturgical instructions, and personal appeals to house churches indicate that Paul wanted them to be read in the churches as a substitute for his personal apostolic presence, so that the message of the gospel, despite his absence, could be proclaimed in power.

Ernst Fuchs has correctly stated that Paul "wrote reluctantly";[3] his letter was only meant to be a substitute for the living message (*viva vox*) of the gospel. Taken together, these considerations render the Pauline letter an unusual phenomenon. It does not pretend to be "literature" because it does not strive to appeal to all circumstances and all peoples of every age. Thus the Pauline letter, as a literary genre, is different from the "gospel," which lays claim to universal validity. Precisely because the letter has another purpose, it claims not only to be a substitute for the immediate dialogue with the apostle's message here and now but it also claims a divine authority comparable to the

3. Fuchs, "Die Sprache im Neuen Testament," 259. Cf. Wilder, *Language*, 22.

prophetic word and the prophetic letter in the Old Testament and in the apocalyptic literature.[4]

Briefly stated, the occasional character of the letters does not suggest that they retain only an occasional value. The letter form, with its combination of particularity and claim to authority, reflects the way Paul does theology. According to Paul, the gospel is a historical entity directed at concrete and contingent situations. The letter must correspond, therefore, to the dialogical form of the gospel and be the substitute for personal, oral communication. The coherent (i.e., lasting and time-enduring) center of the gospel, then, is not an abstraction that can be removed from the context of the immediate audience. Nor is it a universal, timeless substance that can simply be injected into any given historical situation.

Therefore the interpreter should not focus only on the so-called timeless substance and center of the Pauline epistles. On the contrary, the interpreter should concentrate on the concrete, contingent context of a letter. Many interpreters consider a letter's occasion as a purely peripheral problem. Sometimes they even regard the obscurity of a contingent situation as an advantage; for example, the unclear occasion for Romans has been used to justify classifying the letter as a timeless theological treatise.[5] Thus many studies of Pauline theology overlook that the apostle's thought is bound to concrete circumstances and that his various arguments seek to address the requirements of the moment.

The contingent and yet authoritative character of the letters has proved to be a stumbling block for interpreters from the beginning. Where among the diversity of issues and concrete circumstances is the coherence and core of the Pauline message to be found?

The deutero-Pauline letters already sense this problem: How shall Paul's gospel, which lays claim to apostolic

4. For instance, the Jeremiah-Baruch cycle and the letters in the Apocalypse of John.
5. Cf. Nygren, *Commentary on Romans,* 6ff.

authority in quite specific contexts, after the death of the apostle be conveyed to a new generation in which a different thought world predominates. The Pastoral Epistles solve the problem by specifying Paul's "sound teaching" (*hygiainousa didaskalia,* 1 Tim. 1:10; 2 Tim. 4:3) and "the deposit of truth" (*parathēkē,* 1 Tim. 6:20; 2 Tim. 1:12, 14) as the decisive criterion for matters of doctrine and discipline. Ephesians attempts a solution in a speculative way: The author hardly mentions any concrete ecclesiological problems, but rather characterizes Paul as the cornerstone of the church and as the mystagogue of God's revelation through which the church's existence is secured.

Thus it comes as no surprise that, in order to preserve their apostolic authority for the worldwide church, the unique character of the Pauline letters was often ignored. Many have endeavored to skirt this difficult issue by means of an "encyclical hypothesis," according to which Paul in a letter addressed several churches. For example, it has been maintained that Paul wrote Romans as a theological treatise and addressed it to all his churches or for all his churches in certain geographical regions. This "encyclical" letter theory ought to be firmly rejected. It ignores the special character of Paul's letters, resting on the false premise that Paul sent churches theological abstracts of his thought.

When Paul's letters were being collected, their specificity and occasional nature were regarded as a hindrance to their catholicity. Therefore, steps were taken to minimalize their concrete references and to emphasize their universal application and doctrinal uniformity. By way of example, the opening address of 1 Corinthians was expanded in a catholic sense: "together with all those who in every place call on the name of our Lord Jesus Christ, both their Lord and ours" (1 Cor. 1:2). Similarly the closing doxology in Rom. 16:25-27 served to give the letter a "catholic" ending. The particularity of the Pauline letters was even more obscured by the formation of the New Testament canon. The "ecumenical" Paul of Acts, who always proclaims the same message to a variety of churches and remains faithful to the kerygma authorized in Jerusalem, was eventually placed—as a directive to the reader—before the "historical" Paul and his letters. Thus Acts became the key for a correct understanding of Paul's letters, since Acts conveys the impression that the "ecumenical" Paul preaches the same message as well in the letters, which followed Acts. Second Peter also claims that Paul proclaims the "one" catholic message (2 Pet. 3:14-16). The notion of the letters' catholicity was further enhanced when the Catholic Epistles were canonized and placed alongside the Pauline letters. Thus the distinctive voice of the apostle Paul became lost within the harmonious choir of all the apostles. Since the apostolic canon claimed universal relevance, one concluded that Paul (just like the Catholic Epistles) must have addressed himself to all Christian churches. Canonization meant canonicity! Whereas the *plurality* of the Gospels posed a problem for their canonization, as the superscriptions ("the Gospel *according to* . . .") and the popularity of the Diatessaron in the Syrian church indicate, the *particularity* of the Pauline letters posed a similar problem. How was it possible for these letters to claim universal authority for the whole church, when in reality Paul had corresponded with various churches about a whole range of different and specific issues? Plurality and particularity, however, raise the same problem: How can the universality and unity of the gospel be maintained amid the changes of time and circumstance? With respect to the Gospels, Irenaeus speculated that the number four was a universal number. When it came to the Pauline letters, a similar function was claimed for the number seven.[6] Thus Hebrews was listed eventually with the Pauline corpus in order to create a Pauline canon of 2×7.[7] The church, which regarded itself as catholic, solved the problem of the particularity of Paul's letters by playing down their occasional character and by positing their universal significance. The diversity among the individual letters was superceded by

---

6. Cf. the Muratorian Canon (1.69): "they are accepted in the church catholic" ("*in catholica hebentur*").
7. Schmithals, *Paul and the Gnostics*, 266f.

a doctrinal theory of apostolicity, which diffused their particularity. This impugned not only the contingent character of Paul's proclamation of the gospel within the letters but also the specificity of the Pauline gospel within the New Testament canon. Nils Dahl has correctly pointed out that the Muratorian Canon falsely assumes that catholicity does not leave any room for recognizing contingent particularity in the letters of Paul. Instead, he argues, all theology, if it is not to be docetic, must be aware of its own historicity.[8]

The theological tendencies behind the formation of the canon had enormous consequences for the interpretation of Paul's letters. Paul was not only harmonized with the other canonical witnesses, but became as well a witness for doctrinal uniformity. This construction of a catholic Paul yielded disastrous consequences for the understanding of the authentic, "historical" Paul in the church. The catholic Paul is a synthesized Paul, constructed from Acts, the Pauline letters, and the deutero-Pauline letters (Colossians, Ephesians, and the Pastoral Epistles).

It was this Paul who found acceptance in the canon. Nevertheless, one must recognize that the "historical" Paul played hardly a significant role for theology until the time of Augustine and then again in the Reformation.[9] Only since the Reformation has the "historical" Paul again been able to exert a formative influence on the church. This is all the more remarkable when one realizes that the Reformers' grasp of Paul was more intuitive than historical-critical and that they had inherited the centuries-old tradition of a catholic Paul. Since the catholic Paul of the canon was transmitted as a doctrinal authority, the particular and unique elements of Paul's gospel were soon forgotten. The center of Pauline theology was now defined in a doctrinal manner, ignoring the specific circumstances of his letters. Paul's theology was thus handed down from one generation to the next as revealed doctrine.

It becomes clear that such an understanding of the coherence of Paul's gospel simply sacrifices the appreciation

---

8. Dahl, "Particularity," 264, 271.
9. Cf. Lindemann, *Paulus im ältesten Christentum*.

of its contingency. The search for the thematic center of Paul's thought becomes now a search for dogmatic and timeless truth. Such a view dominated Pauline research until the end of the nineteenth century. The alternative to this view, however, was essentially no better: Scholars now focused on Paul's religious experience rather than on Paul's fixed dogma.[10] Both options overlooked the originality of Pauline thought as well as the variability and flexibility of his interpretive method, that is, Paul's unique correlation of universality and particularity, or, as I prefer to state it, the confluence of coherence and contingency. While the search for a "doctrinal" center arrived at an abstract definition, which froze the living language of Paul, the search for an "experiential" center yielded a psychological solution. As a result, a new error was introduced: The "experiential" center could only be discovered *apart from* and *behind* the text. The decisive factor for determining the coherency of Paul's thought was no longer the text itself, but a presupposed(!) religious experience of Paul.

THREE SOLUTIONS

I would like to outline three solutions that have attained a certain prominence in the history of doctrine. I call them (1) the catholic solution, (2) the Marcionite solution, and (3) the psychological solution.

The Catholic Solution. Acts will be used here as the example of the catholic solution, though Colossians, Ephesians, and the Pastoral Epistles also belong to this category. The main contribution of Acts toward solving the problem of contingent diversity in Paul's letters consisted in reducing Paul's thought to a minimum. The distinguishing characteristic of Paul is no longer the originality of his thought, but his remarkable missionary career with its great success. In Acts the eminence of his person legitimizes Paul's apostolic authority. Therefore, primary attention is shifted from the kerygma to the apostleship of Paul. The message of Paul is not what evokes admiration—at least this is not

10. So, e.g., Deissmann, *Paul: A Study in Social and Religious History.*

presented as his distinguishing mark—but rather his distinctive personality.

We must not forget that Paul, as Luke describes him, is not a writer of letters at all. Luke is completely silent on this point. John Knox has observed correctly that "the Paul of the letters is a great letter writer and a poor speaker (2 Cor. 10:10), whereas the Paul of Acts is a great speaker and no letter writer at all."[11] Because Paul's own theology does not play a significant role in Acts, Luke is unable to give Paul's thought any distinctive character. All his speeches follow a similar pattern and resemble "the apostolic kerygma";[12] they are especially similar to the speeches of Peter. This diminution of Paul's specific way of thinking became a part of the later catholic solution and so diffuses the particularity and contingency of Paul's way of doing theology. Moreover, during the period of its controversy with Gnosticism, the church silenced Paul's thought because Gnosticism appealed in some way to Paul. In fact, Paul the theologian was accorded virtually no prominence until Augustine, and he was an exception. Otherwise, the catholic solution prevailed until the Reformation. Although Paul's letters were collected early and were subsequently canonized, and although they were read in the churches, quoted[13] and alluded to,[14] they only had a negligible theological[15] impact. Thus the thought of the apostle was reduced and domesticated to a minimum for the sake of harmonizing his witness with that of the other apostles, with the result that Paul's theological influence in the patristic period was minimal. The silence of the Apologists shows that they regarded Paul as alien, if not dangerous, to their interests. Those interests were directed elsewhere. The teachings of Jesus—the *Nomos*—and the stoic idea of the *Logos* were compatible enough to build a bridge from

11. Knox, *Chapters in a Life of Paul*, 92.
12. Dodd, *The Apostolic Preaching and Its Developments*, 17ff.
13. Cf. Polycarp, *Philippians* 1:1, 3; 3:2; 5:3, and 11:2.
14. Cf. *1 Clement* 5:6; 13:1; 24:1; 34:8; 35:5, 6; 37:5; 47:1-3; and Ignatius, *Ephesians* 1:1; 2:1; 8:2; *Magnesians* 2:1; 10:2; *Trallians* 2:3; 5:1, 2; 10:1; *Romans* 4:3 and 5:1.
15. Cf. 2 Pet. 3:15-16.

the *logos* in every human being to the preexisting *logos* of Christ.

The Marcionite Solution. In contrast to the catholic solution, which features Paul's person and apostolic greatness but harmonizes his thought with that of the New Testament canon as a whole, the "dogmatic" solution focuses on the center and unity of Paul's thought. All else is here regarded as peripheral. An impressive example of this approach is Marcion. With the help of a hermeneutical method consisting of emendation and a falsification theory, he limited the New Testament canon to ten Pauline letters and the Gospel of Luke. He ventured to track down the true Pauline doctrine, which he claimed the Judaizers had perverted. And so he gave Galatians priority of place, while the edited versions of Galatians and Romans became the center of his canon. It was the genius of Marcion that he tried to find a center within the variety of Paul's letters. In this context we must recall, however, the words of Franz Overbeck: Paul "only had one pupil who understood him, Marcion, and he misunderstood him"![16] Marcion's intent was actually rather close to Paul's. Like Paul, he wanted to identify the true gospel of Christ amid the theological diversity of the early church.

In later times, especially since the Enlightenment, Marcion has served as a model for Pauline scholarship as it has searched for the core and center of Pauline thought. Ferdinand Christian Baur, for instance, posited a "Pauline" antithesis to the "Petrine" thesis in order to track down the authentic Paul.[17] Not many years later, William Wrede characterized Paul's theology as "polemical doctrine" (*Kampflehre*),[18] and Albert Schweitzer was convinced that a "primary crater" of eschatalogical mysticism and a secondary crater of rabbinic teaching could be found in the Pauline letters.[19] One must remember, however, that the

16. Overbeck, *Christentum und Kultur*, 218–19. Cf. Harnack, *History of Dogma* 1:89.
17. Baur, *Paul, the Apostle* 1:109–51.
18. Wrede, *Paul*, 74ff.
19. Schweitzer, *The Mysticism of Paul the Apostle*, 205–26.

unity of thought ascribed to Paul by Marcion and his successors is actually in many ways an arbitrary construction.
Here, too, scholars ignored the diversity and occasionality
of Paul's theology.

The error of Marcion and his successors was not so much
the search for a Pauline center but the inability to relate
the core of Paul's thought to the contingency of his letters.
In this way a systematization of Paul could be centered
around a few main concepts, giving others less serious
consideration (see chapter 2). Linguistic categories became
increasingly important as the criterion for interpreting Pauline theology. For example, his thought was divided into
rabbinic and Hellenistic elements in order to arrive at a
reliable core of Paul's theology. It seemed as though Paul
had simply applied a static dogmatic center to the various
historical situations of his churches. The letters of Paul,
however, demand an interpretation that can adequately
explain the correlation between their contingency and
coherence.

Therefore, we learn from the dogmatic-Marcionite solution that a priori judgments concerning what is central
and peripheral do not do justice to Paul's message. Such
an approach can only lead to emendation and selectivity.
The nature of Pauline theology cannot be grasped by a
theory imposed from the outside, which avoids the contingency of the letters and at the same time finds in them
a doctrinal unity.

The Psychological Solution.   A third attempt to come to
terms with the problem of contingency and coherence is
the psychological solution. It takes in essence a developmental hypothesis as its point of departure.

This approach originated as a reaction to the doctrinal
("catholic" or "dogmatic") treatment of Pauline thought.
Heinrich Weinel, Adolf Deissman, and Johannes Schneider,
for example, endeavored to free Paul's religious personality
from sterile, dogmatic categories of thought.[20] Yet the psychological approach, however correct and attractive it may

20. Weinel, *Die Wirkungen des Geistes und der Geister;* Deissmann, *Paul;*
Schneider, *Die Passionsmystik des Paulus.*

be and however popular its method is today in the United States and in Germany,[21] poses a problem. It does indeed account for the variety of Paul's letters. However, this approach can attain a core in Paul's thought only by locating that core in his "pretextual" psyche, that is, in his religious personality. Moreover, the diversity of Paul's thinking is here attributed to his psycho-religious development, which can supposedly be traced in analogy to the chronology reflected by the letters themselves.

Such a developmental scheme has momentous consequences for the description of Paul's eschatology, Christology, and ecclesiology. Thus C. H. Dodd, for example, believes that a line of development can be traced from the earlier future eschatology of Paul to an apparently mature and climactic expression of ecclesiology in Colossians and Ephesians. According to Dodd, the Jewish apocalyptic eschatology became, over a period of time, replaced by the concept of a "divine commonwealth."[22] The psychological solution certainly does respect the diversity of Pauline thought and avoids the arbitrary imposition of an artificial doctrinal system. But the "proof" of an evolution in Paul's thought must remain hypothetical, especially when one considers that the entire Pauline correspondence was produced within six or seven years and that it followed upon at least fifteen years of nonliterary apostolic activity (Galatians 1; 2).

SUMMARY

Each of the three solutions described above has advantages and disadvantages.

The "catholic" perspective focuses on Paul's apostolic activity and on the ecumenical concern for unity within the apostolic canon of the New Testament. But it overlooks the diversity and originality of Paul's thought.

21. Hübner, *Law in Paul's Thought;* Schnelle, "Der erste Thessalonicherbrief und die Entstehung der paulinischen Anthropologie"; Buck and Taylor, *Saint Paul.*
22. Dodd, *The Meaning of Paul for Today.*

The "dogmatic-Marcionite" perspective justifiably in-
tends to recover the specificity and center of Paul's thought.
Its results, however, are ultimately arbitrary, since they
can be reached only through emendation, selectivity, and
a priori doctrinal decisions.

The psychological approach rightly attempts to do justice to the diversity of Paul's thought. Nevertheless, the
construal of a development within Paul's thought must
remain purely conjectural. Moreover, this solution risks
the danger of disregarding the text of the letters for the
sake of constructing a speculative "psychological" center.

All three solutions overlook a most important point: the
correlation between contingency and coherence in Paul's
thought. Thus a reconsideration of "Paul's interpretation
of the gospel" is called for.

2

Primary Themes
in Pauline Thought

Two major themes dominate Paul's thought: (1) the dialectic of coherence and contingency and (2) the apocalyptic worldview as the basic framework of Paul's gospel.

THE DIALECTIC OF COHERENCE
AND CONTINGENCY

The coherence-contingency scheme rests on the supposition that Paul is neither a systematic theologian (as Marcion thought) nor a successful missionary (as Acts describes him), but foremost an exegete. An adequate interpretation of Paul must focus on the character and function of his hermeneutical reflections, that is, on his specific thought structure, without which all other facets of his theology cannot be solved.

My thesis claims that Paul's interpretation of the gospel consists of a complicated interplay between coherence and contingency. By *coherence* I mean the unchanging components of Paul's gospel, which contain the fundamental convictions of his gospel: Paul himself calls them "the truth of the gospel" (Gal. 2:5, 14), and threatens those who would pervert them with an apocalyptic curse (Gal. 1:8, 9; cf. Phil. 1:27; cf. 2 Thess. 1:8; 2:2).

The term *contingency* denotes the changing, situational part of the gospel, that is, the diversity and particularity of sociological, economical, and psychological factors that confront Paul in his churches and in his missionary work and to which he had to respond.

Paul's proclamation focuses on the interplay between coherence and contingency in response to the question, How can the truth of the gospel be proclaimed in such a way that it fulfills its intended purpose in concrete situations? For this reason it is necessary to be always mindful of the interaction between fundamental content and situational context. For content not only influences context, but it is also shaped by context.

Paul's hermeneutic not only extrapolates a specific core from the rich diversity of ecclesial gospel traditions, but also concretizes this core in such a manner that it can become a word on target for every particular historical context. Because Paul is able to combine particularity and universality, diversity and uniformity, the gospel is neither reduced to an orthodox, timeless system nor to a series of disconnected and incidental thoughts.

In this context it is important to notice that the "coherent center" of Paul's thought becomes diluted into an abstract and powerless system whenever it is severed from its concrete context. Conversely, the hermeneutic of Paul disintegrates into an opportunistic and arbitrary scheme whenever the contingent character of the gospel loses its connection with the coherent core, that is, with its solid foundation.

My discussion in chapter 1 concerning the nature of Paul's letters makes clear that the specific character of the letter fits in well with the interplay between coherence and contingency. This dynamic interplay in the letters also illuminates the distinctive character of Paul's hermeneutic. Paul's hermeneutical versatility reflects a creative freedom that adapts the gospel tradition and shapes it into a living word within the varied circumstances of his churches.

The "core" of the gospel for Paul is not a static message that can simply be imposed as fixed doctrine on contingent circumstances. But, conversely, it cannot simply be accommodated to whatever the situation demands. For Paul tradition is always *interpreted tradition,* formulated in the freedom of the Spirit.

My thesis claims, therefore, that the uniqueness (the *proprium*) of Paul's hermeneutic manifests itself in the interplay between the changing and unchanging elements of the gospel. Paul is capable of transforming the gospel into a living word in various contexts without, on the whole, compromising the totality of the gospel or without trivializing the specific particularities that each situation demands. Paul's commitment to the truth of the gospel and to its concrete effectiveness clearly shows the interaction between coherence and contingency.

The power (*dynamis*) of the gospel is for Paul the confirmation of its truth (*alētheia;* cf. Gal. 2:5, 14). But the reverse also holds true: Since the gospel is true, it demonstrates itself as an active power (Rom. 1:16; 1 Cor. 1:18-25). Therefore, the effective power and the truth of the gospel belong together in a dialectic tension: They are inseparable, since for Paul the gospel contains both constant truth and dynamic power.

On the one hand the power of the gospel is manifest in the very existence of churches, which are the "fruit" of Paul (Rom. 1:13; 15:28): "his glory and joy" (1 Thess. 2:20), "joy and crown" (Phil. 4:1), "the seal of my apostleship" (1 Cor. 9:2) and the reason for his boast "in the day of Christ that I did not run in vain or labor in vain" (Phil. 2:16). In 1 Thess. 1:5 Paul emphatically underlines the concrete effectiveness of the gospel: "for our preaching came to you not only in word alone, but also in power and in the Holy Spirit and with full conviction." On the other hand, the power of the gospel depends on its truth, that is, on its specific identity as the gospel "of Jesus Christ and him crucified" (1 Cor. 2:2), "besides whom there is no other gospel" (Gal. 1:6, 7; 2 Cor. 11:4). The interplay between the *truth* and *power* of the gospel helps explain the amazing relationship between the content of the gospel and its effective-contingent explication. The coherent center and its varied explanations are not related in the way a code of law is related to its casuistic interpretation or in the way dogmatic propositions require new application. On the contrary, they are related in such a manner that the crucified and risen Lord (1 Cor. 2:2; Rom. 8:34) foreshadows the final triumph of God within the particular historical circumstances of the individual churches.

As I have already mentioned, the letter form is for Paul and his theological method an emergency measure, because it represents a substitute for his personal presence and his dialogical, oral communication. Therefore, the letter is not a dogmatic text or static tradition that can now become the subject of a systemic treatment of the Christian faith, as if it were simply a series of theological propositions. And yet the letter is not simply an accidental item as if its occasional character represented an obstacle for sketching Paul's theology. And so the critical issue arises: Are we able to cull Paul's theology from the specific and immediate occasions of the letters? Or do we have to generalize their statements, so that they degenerate into a series of theological propositions or doctrinal themes?

For Paul theological thinking and theological method go hand in hand. His gospel is therefore gospel because his thought and method have a practical objective. For this reason Paul's gospel cannot be reduced to a philosophically abstract structure. Thought leads to praxis and praxis evokes thought. Paul's hermeneutic is a combination of both! In this respect it resembles the method of the "liberation theology" of Central and South America, where theological reflection is based on the concrete circumstances of the church in society.

The mutual interaction between the coherent center of the gospel and its concrete, contingent application has a further consequence for the study of Paul: As long as key concepts are examined in isolation from one another, his kerygma cannot be understood. For such key terms in and of themselves do not represent the core of the gospel. Concepts such as "the righteousness of God," "justification," "salvation," or "reconciliation" cannot be played off against each other, as if one of them were decisive for explaining the meaning of all the others. Instead, all these terms are metaphors that must make the gospel effective and, therefore, significant for particular situations.

Thus the coherent center of Paul's thought cannot be comprehended by one concept alone. We must instead become aware of this coherent center as *a field* of meaning, a network composed of parts that interlock in a symbolic relationship. The makeup of this field as a whole is determined by the apocalyptic act of God in the death and resurrection of Christ.

We will see as well that the dialogical scheme of coherence and contingency has important consequences for the apostolate of Paul.

APOCALYPTIC AS THE BASIS OF PAUL'S GOSPEL

Jewish apocalyptic forms the basis of Paul's thought. It constituted (*a*) the thought world of Paul the Pharisee and, therefore, (*b*) the fundamental grammar and context through which Paul filtered the Christ event and interpreted it as the *apokalypsis tou christou* (Gal. 1:12; cf. 1:16; 2:2). The co-incidence of "conversion" and "apostolic call" in the Damascus experience (Gal. 1:15) shows that "the truth of the gospel," that is, the apocalyptic interpretation of the cross and the resurrection of Christ, provided not only the solution for Paul's own personal and contingent crisis but also the abiding answer for the manifold crisis situations that confronted his communities.

My thesis that Jewish apocalyptic determined the symbolic framework of Paul's thought does not mean that Paul used Jewish apocalyptic as a literary genre or employed Jewish apocalypses as a literary source. Similarly, I am not interested in undertaking a semantic study of the concept "apocalyptic" in relation to Paul.[1] Rather, I claim that Jewish apocalyptic *motifs* dominate Paul's thought. The influence Paul exerted on Christian tradition was not so much

1. See Keck, "Paul and Apocalyptic Theology."

the result of Hellenistic-Jewish or Philonic ideas as of a
Jewish apocalyptic way of thinking.

The coherence of the gospel actually consists of the apocalyptic interpretation of the death and resurrection of
Christ. In this respect William Wrede taught us that in
Paul "all statements about salvation as an accomplished
fact are immediately transformed into statements about the
future."[2] Along similar lines, I argue that the coherence of
the gospel is constituted by statements that have been
shaped by apocalyptic thought and, consequently, cannot
be separated from their ultimate goal, the imminent apocalyptic triumph of God.

The significance of apocalyptic for Paul may be outlined
as follows:

1. The enduring center of Paul's gospel is his conviction
that Christ's death and resurrection have opened up a new
future for the world. This future will reach its climax when
the reign and triumph of God are made manifest and the
whole created order attains its wonderful perfection according to God's promises to Israel.

2. The apocalyptic framework of the gospel also cor-
responds to the manner in which Paul proclaims it. The
gospel concerning the future reign of God is brought to
expression in such a way that, analogous to the incarnation
of God in Christ, it embodies itself in the concrete and
varied circumstances of human life. In this way Paul enables
his churches to discern already in the present time signs of
God's future glory. Moreover, Paul's churches are empow-
ered by God to participate in redemptive praxis in the
world, which aims at preparing the whole creation for its
future glory.

Paul borrows certain components of his apocalyptic gospel from the Jewish apocalyptic thought world, but he
modifies them because of his encounter with the exalted
Christ and through the influence of the Christian tradition.

Although this is not the place to describe the general
character of apocalyptic, the central question apocalyptic

2. Wrede, *Paul*, 105-6.

poses is quite clear: Why is faithfulness to the God of the covenant and to the Torah rewarded with persecution and suffering? Apocalyptic is an attempt to overcome the discrepancy between the harsh realities of everyday life and the promises of God. Though Paul strongly modifies the imagery and conceptuality of apocalyptic, his thought is molded by four central motifs of Jewish apocalyptic: (1) the faithfulness and vindication of God, (2) the universal salvation of the world, (3) the dualistic structure of the world, and (4) the imminent coming of God in glory.

The Faithfulness and Vindication of God

Paul's interpretation of the gospel is an interpretation in the perspective of hope because he believes in the God of Israel, who has confirmed his self-vindication and faithfulness to his promises in the death and resurrection of Jesus Christ and will soon bring them to fulfillment in his whole creation. These promises pertain to the yet-awaited public manifestation of the reign of God: the visible presence of God in the midst of his people, the destruction of all his enemies, and the vindication of Israel in the gospel.

The death and resurrection of Jesus Christ reveal the enduring faithfulness and ultimate vindication of God. As Ernst Käsemann has shown, the righteousness of God in Paul means not only God's gift in Christ to the church, but also the sovereign claim of the creator over his world.[3] In the Old Testament it is especially the Psalms and Ezekiel that bind God to his promises:

> For thy name's sake, O Lord, preserve my life! In thy righteousness bring me out of trouble! And in your steadfast love cut off my enemies. May all my opponents perish! (Ps. 143:11–12a)

> Therefore thus says the Lord God: "Now I will restore the fortunes of Jacob, and have mercy upon the whole house of Israel; and I will be jealous for my holy name." (Ezek. 39:25; cf. 39:7, 21)

3. Käsemann, " 'The Righteousness of God,' " in *Perspectives on Paul,* 178–82.

"It is not for your sake, O house of Israel, that I am about
to act, but for the sake of my holy name, which you have
profaned among the nations to which you came. And I
will vindicate the holiness of my great name, which has
been profaned among the nations and which you have
profaned among them. And the nations," says the Lord
God, "will know that I am the Lord, when through you
I vindicate my holiness before their eyes." (Ezek. 36:22–
23)

We must keep in mind that these statements belong to
Israel's postexilic context, when serious questions were
being raised concerning the faithfulness of God: Why does
God reward Israel's faithfulness with persecution, death,
and suffering? Is not it a fact of experience that the enemies
of God and not the God of Israel control the affairs of the
world? In this context of longing for the vindication of
God's power over his world, Paul proclaims the gospel of
Jesus Christ as the inauguration of God's faithfulness. Thus
Paul proclaims in 2 Cor. 1:20, "For all the promises of God
find their Yes in him. That is why we utter the Amen
through him, to the glory of God." Paul presents here
Christ as the revelation of the *Amen* of God,[4] that is, as
the symbol of God's faithfulness to his promises. Paul's
christological proclamation cannot be simply fitted into a
promise-fulfillment scheme, as if Christ, the "Yes" of God,
were the climax of God's self-vindication. We must, indeed, avoid such a spiritualizing of the eschatological
promise; the self-vindication of God and his faithfulness
to Israel do not occur in a scheme that leaves the structures
of the history of the world untouched. In order to resist
such a misunderstanding, Paul insists that the present gift
of the Spirit is not the full payment of God's promises,
but rather their guarantee (2 Cor. 1:22). Thus one must
not, for all the importance of Christology in Paul's message, forget the theocentric, that is, the God-centered texture of his thought. Romans 4:17 confirms this: Abraham
is said to stand "in the presence of the God in whom he

4. *Amen* is the Hebrew word corresponding to the Greek *to nai* = "yes."

believed, who gives life to the dead and calls into existence the things that do not exist." God is here described as the creator and eschatological redeemer, the one whose sovereignty at the beginning of creation will be confirmed by the vindication of his sovereignty at the end of creation (cf. 2 Cor. 1:19).

The theocentric character of Paul's thought is further confirmed by the "faithful" clauses of his letters: "He who calls you is faithful, and he will do it" (1 Thess. 5:24); "God, by whom you were called into the fellowship of his son, Jesus Christ our Lord, is faithful" (1 Cor. 1:9; 2 Cor. 1:18).[5] This is the reason the "faithlessness" of Israel cannot "nullify the faithfulness of God" (Rom. 3:3), that is, God's self-vindication: "By no means! Let God be true though every man be false" (Rom. 3:4a). Paul would have agreed with the author of Revelation when he described God as "the Alpha and the Omega . . . who is and who was and who is to come, the ruler over all creation" (Rev. 1:8). And with the twenty-four elders of the Apocalypse Paul would have sung, "Thou art worthy, our Lord and God, to receive glory and honor and power, for thou didst create all things, and by thy will they existed and were created" (Rev. 4:11). Finally, Paul would have concurred with Rev. 11:15: "The kingdom of the world has now become the kingdom of our Lord and his anointed one; and they shall reign throughout eternity."

The faith of the Christian community is anchored in God's overarching plan of redemption. It is God who alone will execute this plan and who alone determined the "fullness of time" (Gal. 4:4), in which his Son appeared to inaugurate the liberation of the created order. This is why the church responds with an "Amen" to the Yes (= Amen) of God's act in Christ (cf. 2 Cor. 1:20). Faith (*pistis*) can be characterized simply as a "Yes" to the faithfulness of God (*pistis*), which in Rom. 3:3 is strikingly formulated in a negative way: "Does their [Israel's] faithlessness [*apistia*]

---

5. Cf. Osten-Sacken, "Gottes Treue bis zur Parusie."

nullify the faithfulness [*pistis*] of God?" In fact, God's trust-worthiness forms the basis of the confidence and trust of the church: "I am confident that he who began a good work in you will bring it to completion on the day of Jesus Christ" (Phil. 1:6).

In fact, in Paul's letters faith regularly spills over into hope (Rom. 4:18; 5:3-5; 8:25; Gal. 5:5; 1 Thess. 1:3). The framework of apocalyptic eschatology in which Paul stands becomes especially clear in his frequent use of terms such as "endurance," "patience," "perseverance" and "longing" (see Rom. 2:4; 5:3, 4; 8:25; 15:5; Gal. 5:22; 2 Cor. 6:4, 6; 1 Thess. 1:3, 4). These terms are interrelated because they are all concerned with the object of the hope, that is, with the vindication of God at the end of time. Thus faith and hope are synonymous concepts, not only because they delineate a disposition of trust but also because they are directed to the one focus and object of this trust, the coming reign of God.

"Faith in (Jesus) Christ," then, is an abbreviation for "faith in the God, who in Christ's death and resurrection has redeemed us from the bondage of sin and has trans-ferred us to the dominion of his righteousness."[6] Paul char-acterizes Jesus Christ as the pledge of God's imminent self-vindication. Faith in Christ manifests that reality of hope which is able to bear the tension between our confession of God's righteousness and the concrete, unredeemed re-ality of the present world.

In short, Paul's gospel is rooted in a theocentric (that is, a God-centered) worldview. Paul joins apocalyptic to this theocentric perspective. Consequently, the promises of the Old Testament have not been "fulfilled" in the gospel of Christ and should therefore not be spiritualized. Rather they are taken up in the gospel so as to evoke a new expectation and hope for their ultimate "fulfillment" in the kingdom of God.

6. Cf. Rom. 3:21-26.

Universalism

The theme of God's faithfulness and self-vindication is closely related to the apocalyptic motif of the universal reign of God. Universalism signifies the depth and cosmic breadth of the vindication of God as the vindication of all creation. God plans to demonstrate his vindication only through the eschatological liberation of his entire creation: "Then the glory of the Lord will be revealed, and all people shall see it" (Isa. 40:5). "For as the earth makes seed grow and as a garden brings forth plants, so also the Lord God will cause righteousness and praise to spring forth before all nations" (Isa. 61:11).

In the combination of these two themes of vindication and universalism we can discern the difference between Paul's view of cosmic universalism and that of Judaism. Cosmic universalism—or the worldwide extension of God's majesty and glory—is radically modified by Paul. In Jewish apocalyptic the faithfulness and vindication of God is primarily directed to the vindication of those in Israel who are obedient to the Law of God. For this reason Israel's hope is concerned first of all with its own relief from suffering at the hands of its enemies. And even when Israel views the messianic era in terms of a pilgrimage of the gentile nations to Jerusalem (Isa. 2:2-3; Mic. 4:1-2), Israel's thinking remains introverted. Although Israel can conceive of a new covenant with God in the messianic era, it finds the notion of a new Torah or its abrogation abhorrent. Thus there is a close connection between the identity of Israel as a people and God's apocalyptic vindication. "The dividing wall of the law" (Eph. 2:14) marks Israel's ethnocentricity: It signifies a sharp distinction between us, "the insiders," and them, "the outsiders."

Paul modifies this apocalyptic motif at its very foundation. He does not draw a dividing line between those faithful to the Torah and gentile "sinners" (Gal. 2:15), but marks the death of Jesus Christ as the focal point of God's universal wrath and judgment. He understands the death of Christ as the apocalyptic judgment on all people, while

Christ's resurrection signifies the free gift of new life in
Christ for all (Rom 5:12-19). Thus there cannot be any
favorite-nation clause or claim to special privilege before
the apocalyptic judgment of God by appealing to the cross
of Christ. Although this radicalization of the human condition in the cross of God's Messiah logically carries the
idea of a universal salvation, Paul refrains from making
such an assertion. The time between the cross/resurrection
and the end is a time for commitment, mission, endurance,
and obedience. Those who are disobedient to the gospel
will be judged and destroyed in the last judgment, for they
continue to behave as though the powers defeated by Jesus
Christ are still in charge. Thus Paul balances the notion of
a universal salvation with an emphasis on the responsibility
and obedience of those who have heard the gospel.

In addition to his rejection of elitism, Paul emphasizes
three further aspects concerning God's universalism. He
interprets the cosmic-universal rule of God in the context
of (1) a cosmic anthropology and of (2) a cosmic righteousness, and hence of (3) a concrete ethic of solidarity.

Käsemann has correctly identified the essential elements
of cosmic righteousness and anthropology in Paul: "We
are always what we are in the mode of belongingness and
participation, whether as friend or foe, whether in thinking, acting, or suffering. The ontological statement of Pauline anthropology is crystallized in its ontic conclusions:
man is always himself in his particular world; his being is
open towards all sides and is always set in a structure of
solidarity." "Anthropology is cosmology *in concreto,* even
in the sphere of faith."[7] Since the human being is placed
within the power structures of the world and thus must
be viewed from a cosmological perspective, there is a profound solidarity and interdependence not only among the
people of the world, but also between my "inner world,"
my "social world," and my "ecological world."[8] God,

7. Käsemann, *Perspectives on Paul,* 21, 22, and 27.
8. These terms ("Eigenwelt," "Mitwelt," and "Umwelt") are taken from
Ludwig Binswanger, "Über Psychotherapie."

therefore, will only then be vindicated and people will only then be fully saved when God's whole creation attains its glorious destiny. Thus the universal and comprehensive reign of God signifies the depth and breadth of God's self-vindication which will only come about when the whole world is vindicated.

Dualism

Paul uses two further apocalyptic motifs in his proclamation of the gospel. The motifs of God's faithfulness, vindication, and universalism, that I discussed above, call attention to the theocentric nature of Paul's gospel. The motifs of *dualism* and *imminence* specify the power of the Spirit in the present situation of the Christian community. The Christian community is not only involved in the oppressive structures of a godless world but is also motivated by an intense hope in God's final hour of redemption.

The apocalyptic motif of dualism emphasizes that God, in his plan of salvation *for* the world, calls Christians to fight *against* the present power structures of the world. Paul employs the motif of dualism to focus attention on the hope that is based on God's victory in Christ and that incarnates itself for Christians in a cruciform existence, that is, in a life under the cross.

Dualism describes not only the powers—the structures of evil—that attempt to thwart the universal vindication of God's plan of salvation, it also describes the provisional anticipation of God's vindication—the power of the Spirit—in our midst. In Jewish apocalyptic the motif of dualism expresses the antithesis between the present and future world, that is, the enmity between the evil powers of the world and the representatives of the kingdom of God to come. This antithesis is rooted in a deep existential concern and in many ways reflects a theology of martyrdom. The Jewish apocalypticist experiences a profound contradiction between his loyalty to the Torah and its apparent futility. His hope, which is contradicted by the stubborn realities of the world, is nurtured by faith in God's

faithfulness and ultimate self-vindication. The dualism between "this age" and "the age to come" is to be understood
in relation to the cosmic anthropology of apocalyptic.[9] The
forces of evil that dominate the present world are both
macrocosmic and microcosmic. The angelic forces under
the rule of Satan are in control not only of the world of
history but also of the inner being of persons. In the coming
kingdom of God both humankind and nature will be radically transformed, so that they will participate in God's
glory, that is, in God's vindication of his creation.

However, Paul's Christian form of apocalyptic modifies
this Jewish–dualistic motif by tempering it (Ia + b), on
the one hand, and by intensifying it (II), on the other.

(Ia) Paul tempers the dualism between the present age
and the age to come by interpreting the history of Israel
in a typological way. The era of "the old covenant" had
its own temporary "glory" (2 Cor. 3:7-11); the exodus
story takes on eschatological significance for Christians (1
Cor. 10:1-13); the privileges of Israel are real and abiding
(Romans 9–11) and play an essential role in the history of
salvation.

(Ib) Furthermore, the death and resurrection of Christ
mark the incursion of the future age into the old age. Thus
the Christ-event has considerably modified the dualistic
structure of Jewish apocalyptic thought. The power of the
new age is already at work in the church and empowers
Christians to resist the "deeds of the body" (Rom. 8:13),
since the pledge of the new age, the Holy Spirit, is already
present in their midst. The Spirit enables "a new creation"
to occur in the midst of the old creation (2 Cor. 5:17) and
manifests itself in "signs, wonders, and mighty works" (2
Cor. 12:12; cf. Rom. 15:17-19) and in glossolalia, prophecy,
and healings (1 Cor. 12:4-11).

Paul tempers the dualism between this and the coming
age, then, by emphasizing continuity in the midst of discontinuity, a continuity that is grounded in God's faithfulness to Israel. Furthermore, the proleptic experience of

9. As n. 7 above.

the new age is manifest in the new life in the Spirit made possible for Christians through the death and resurrection of Jesus Christ.

(II) From another perspective, however, dualism is sharply intensified. Since the forces of the future are already at work in the world, the confrontation in the present world between the powers of death and the powers of life aggravates the crisis. Christian existence in the world makes this clear. Just as the *universalistic* motif compels the church to adopt a radical stance *for* the world, the *dualistic* motif compels the church do battle *against* the godless world—all the more so because this struggle has its foundation in the cross of Christ, which represents God's radical "No" to the value structures of our world. The "rulers of the world" (1 Cor. 2:8) have not only crucified Christ but continue to crucify those who belong to Christ (2 Cor. 4:7-12). The church signifies the dawning of the new world of God in the midst of the old age and is like a heavenly vanguard that fights against the forces of evil. Paul deals with the theme of the church *over against* the world in several ways: it is the battle of the Spirit (*pneuma*) against the flesh (*sarx;* Gal. 5:17), of faith in Christ against the dominion of the law (Gal. 2:15-21), of the foolishness of the cross against the wisdom of the world (1 Cor. 1:18-25) and, last but not least, the battle between the powers of life against the powers of death (Rom. 8:38-39). In the midst of this battle, there is necessary suffering: not only suffering to be endured passively, because of the onslaught of the powers of this world, but also suffering as a result of active Christian engagement with the world, because the church has a redemptive mission *in* the world *for* the world in accordance with the redemptive plan of God in Christ. Thus the church lives in a continuous tension between being for the world and being against the world. In this situation the church is threatened by two dangers. First, if it emphasizes too strongly withdrawal from the world in a dualistic fashion, it threatens to become a purely sectarian apocalyptic movement that forfeits God's redemptive plan for the whole world in the death and resurrection of Christ. Second, if the church exclusively emphasizes participation in the world, it threatens to become another "worldly" phenomenon, accommodating itself to whatever the world will buy and so becoming a part of the world.

There is, however, a suprapersonal, cosmic dimension to the suffering of the church. Ephesians describes this dimension this way: "For we are not contending against flesh and blood, but against the principalities, against the powers, against the world rulers of this present darkness, against the spiritual hosts of wickedness in the heavenly places" (Eph. 6:12). Although Paul, unlike Ephesians, rarely enumerates the transcendent inhabitants of the heavenly world, his own view accords with the apocalyptic sentiment of Ephesians: Behind the manifestations of human sin lies a complex network of evil that is constituted by the powers of the "flesh," of the "law," of "sin," and of "death." This network of evil operates as an interrelated whole; it is an alliance of powers under the sovereign and cosmic reign of death. Death is indeed "the last enemy" (1 Cor. 15:26), and until it has been defeated God's final triumph is still outstanding. And so the present reign of death intensifies the suffering of the Christian community. For although Christians participate in the dominion of Christ, "who has conquered death in his resurrection" (Rom. 6:9), and although they are people "who have been brought over from death into life" (Rom. 6:13), nevertheless the power of death is still the signature of existence for both the church and the world. Christians are still subject to death (1 Thess. 4:13), and death still manifests its rule in creation's "bondage to decay" (Rom. 8:21) and "futility" (Rom. 8:20), that is, in "the slings and arrows of outrageous fortune" (Shakespeare).[10] Death exercises its power over the whole creation, in all of its groaning and suffering.

Although Paul teaches in accordance with Jewish apocalyptic tradition that death and suffering are caused by sin (cf. Rom. 5:12), he nevertheless leaves room for the

10. Shakespeare, *Hamlet* 3.1.58.

thought that there is a crucial and mysterious "dark" residue of evil and death in God's created order, which is not the outcome of human sin. Paul is convinced that this evil residue, which causes all sorts of suffering, will be defeated in the hour of God's final triumph. Paul can maintain this conviction since he, despite the fact that he derives death from the sin of Adam in Rom. 5:12-19, in fact emphasizes a crucial difference between Christ and Christians in the realm of salvation. For although *Christ has* defeated *both sin* and *death,* that is, has freed Christians from sin through their participation in him (Rom. 6:1-23), *Christians* are nevertheless still engaged in the battle with death, "the last enemy" (1 Cor. 15:26), which will not be defeated until the return of Christ at the end of time. It is therefore inappropriate to attribute to human sin every form of the power of death in the world—especially those forms of suffering that so often seem utterly meaningless.

Imminence

The apocalyptic motif of imminence or hope in the impending reality of God's reign is closely related to the three motifs discussed above. Paul strengthens the motif of imminence by linking it to an intense hope in the vindication of God and his universal reign.

Ever since the Enlightenment, New Testament scholars have sought to excise the imminent expectation of the end time from Paul's thought. Although many exegetes concede that apocalyptic terminology plays an important role in Pauline theology, its futurist-imminent aspect presents so many problems to our modern way of thinking that it is either demythologized or neutralized in some other way. On the one hand, it is characterized as a flexible variable, while the Christ-event is regarded as the stable center of Paul's thought. On the other hand, imminence is often assigned to "the early Paul"—something he abandoned during his more mature years. The categorization of imminence as a Jewish residue and hence as a mistaken notion of Paul serves as yet another explanation.

There are at least three aspects to the theme of imminence in Paul: its *necessity,* its *unpredictability,* and the *dialectic of patience and impatience.*

Necessity. The expectation of the imminent parousia of Christ and the "day of the Lord" is for Paul not an apocalyptic oddity, but forms the climax of his theological fabric.[11] The impending return of Christ is made necessary by the central significance that Paul assigns to the resurrection of Christ. Whenever Paul mentions the resurrection, he employs apocalyptic language. Resurrection terminology can be understood only in terms of the apocalyptic hope of the universal resurrection of the dead, an event that will coincide with the manifestation of God's full glory. Paul proclaims the necessary connection between the resurrection of Christ and the final resurrection of the dead. Accordingly, Paul presents Christ as "the first fruits of those who are asleep" (1 Cor. 15:23) or as "the firstborn among many brethren to come" (Rom. 8:29).

Thus the Christ-event in and of itself is not the final climax or a closure event. The expression "first fruits" signifies that time strains toward its actualization in the harvest of the final resurrection of the dead. The connection between the resurrection of Christ and God's final triumph is confirmed by Paul's view of the Spirit. As Christ is related to the general resurrection, so also is the Holy Spirit related to the coming glory of God. In fact, the Spirit, according to Paul, is the agent of the future glory of God in the present; it is the first down payment (Rom. 8:23) or the guarantee (2 Cor. 1:22) of the end time and thus the signal of its coming and of God's imminent triumph.

The Spirit, as the vanguard of the Kingdom's power, battles against the power of the flesh and in so doing moves Christians in the direction of the future from which the Spirit comes, that is, the future of God's glory. It comes therefore as no surprise that Paul uses military and promissory images to convey the Spirit's activity in the here and

11. As n. 2 above.

now. The church eagerly awaits the coming of Christ because there is a contradiction between its empirical existence in the world and the promise epitomized in the resurrection of Christ. The cry of the martyrs under the altar in Revelation, "O Sovereign Lord, holy and true, how long before thou wilt judge and avenge our blood on those who dwell upon the earth" (Rev. 6:10) echoes in many ways the petition "Maranatha"—"Our Lord, come!" (1 Cor. 11:26)—uttered in Paul's churches. Likewise, Paul exhorts the Philippians: "I am sure that he who began a good work in you will bring it to completion at the day of Jesus Christ" (Phil. 1:6).

The imminence motif is much more intense in Paul's letters than in Jewish apocalyptic, since the death and resurrection of Christ alrcady heralds the incursion of the future into the present. Christ, who has come "in the fullness of time" (Gal. 4:4), has inaugurated the end of time so that after his death and resurrection no eschatological timetable needs to be established, and in principle no other conditions need to be met before his glorious return in the triumph of God.

And so the apocalyptic themes of *vindication, universalism,* and *dualism* are all embraced by the intensity of the hope in the universal and cosmic reign of God that will dissolve all dualistic structures of the world and eliminate all suffering. The antiphony of Revelation (chapter 22) might as well have been taken from the liturgy of one of Paul's churches: "The Spirit and the Bride say, 'Come.' And let him who hears say, 'Come' (v. 17). 'Surely I am coming soon.' Amen. Come, Lord Jesus!" (v. 20). Indeed, at that time Paul's hope will be realized: "I consider that the sufferings of this present time are not worth comparing with the glory that is to be revealed to us" (Rom. 8:18).

Unpredictability. It is impossible to conceive of an authentic Pauline theology without apocalyptic hope. This hope is directed toward the definitive final closure event of history, that is, toward the imminent coming of God and Christ. But we must remember as well that Paul's apocalyptic becomes distorted when that hope becomes the object of human calculation, speculation, and prediction.

Paul is, after all, a writer of letters and not of apocalypses; he uses apocalyptic motifs, but not the literary genre of apocalypse. Paul Hanson has convincingly pointed out that the category of "apocalyptic" contains various forms. It can refer either to a literary *genre,* to a prominent *motif,* or to an apocalyptic *movement.*[12] Thus we should be aware of the fact that Paul uses apocalyptic motifs, but not the literary genre, while his churches evolve into apocalyptic movements. Thus for Paul Christian hope is *a matter of prophecy and not of prediction.* The incalculability of the hope is for Paul one of its essential marks.[13]

Unlike the apocalyptic tendency to project an exact timetable of the "last events," Paul stresses the unpredictability of the end; like other New Testament writings, Paul emphasizes the unexpected, sudden character of the final theophany. At the same time, Paul severely limits the use of apocalyptic language and imagery. In fact, his theology is often characterized as "nonapocalyptic" because, contrary to Revelation and Jewish apocalypses, he shows little interest in heavenly topography and in portraying fantastic scenes of the last judgment or of the heavenly kingdom. For those "upon whom the end of the ages has come" (1 Cor. 10:1) and for those who participate in the powers of the dawning age to come, what else can their attitude be but one of rejoicing in "the God of hope . . . with all joy and peace" (Rom. 15:13)?

Paul, the prophet of God's imminent glory, does not deduce the date of the coming reign of God from a variety of historical events; rather, he deduces from God's promises—confirmed by Christ—the impending nearness of the vindication of God and the fulfillment of his promises.

The imminence of God's universal reign, then, is grounded in a radical faith in the God of the promise and

12. Hanson, "Apocalypticism."
13. Consequently, 2 Thessalonians cannot have been written directly by Paul: Its apocalyptic program is quite unlike the tenor of Paul's authentic letters.

not in a historical determinism, as if the believer could live by speculative knowledge rather than by faith. Thus the delay of the parousia does not constitute a real problem for Paul. It does not compel him to shift the center of his attention away from apocalyptic expectation to a kind of *realized eschatology,* that is, to a conviction of the full presence of the kingdom of God in our present history. One must learn to distinguish in Paul between peripheral and essential changes in his view on imminence. Changes in his perspective that do not touch his basic conviction on the matter occur in 1 Cor. 15:15-51, 2 Cor. 5:1-10, Phil. 1:21-24, and 1 Thess. 4:13-18. However, the hope in the impending reign of God through Christ remains the constant theme and is present in all his letters, from 1 Thessalonians to Romans and Philippians.

The necessity of the imminent end of history and its unpredictability are not mutually exclusive. On the contrary, Paul joins both motifs together. Every attempt to calculate the date of the end of history would reduce the intensity of the hope and would destroy the very character of Christian faith as absolute dependence on the God of hope.

Patience/Impatience. The dialectic of patience and impatience in Paul's apostolic life seems at first glance to be an outright contradiction. For how is it possible for Paul to be engaged in two apparently opposite activities? How can he simultaneously long for the future reign of God and yet be occupied with mapping out a mission strategy for the long run? From what we know about apocalyptic sects, would we not expect an otherworldly attitude, accompanied by ethical passivity, in the knowledge that "the appointed time has grown very short" (1 Cor. 7:29) and that "the form of this world is passing away" (1 Cor. 7:31)? How can Paul combine his passionate hope with his insistence on sobriety (2 Cor. 5:13), endurance, and with his daily pragmatic-pastoral care for all the churches (2 Cor. 11:28)?

This question is all the more crucial since Paul's conviction about the impending end compels him to proclaim a passionate disengagement with the structures of this world (1 Cor. 7:29-31) and a fervent anticipation of the coming glory of God (Rom. 13:11-12; 2 Cor. 12:12).

In other words, how are *passion* and *sobriety* related in his personal life, and how are apostolicity and apocalyptic related in his missionary activity? It is important to recognize that these two dispositions belong together in Paul's life because the *necessity* of the impending end is directly interwoven with its *unpredictability*. This gives Paul the freedom to be committed simultaneously to the expectation of history's end and to the contingencies of historical life. The one who has seen the signs of the coming transformation of the world in the Christ-event and has seen its consequences for the church is able to allow God the freedom to choose the moment of his final glorious theophany. In the meantime Paul strives to move God's world in the direction of its appointed destiny.

There is, then, a passion in Paul, but it is the passion of sobriety; and there is impatience in Paul, but it is an impatience tempered by the patience of preparing the world for its coming glory, which the Christ-event has already inaugurated.

PART TWO

THEOLOGICAL CONSEQUENCES

3

The Contingency of
the Gospel

In chapter 1 I discussed how the form of Paul's letters underscores the contingent nature of his theological thought. Subsequently (chapter 2) I attempted to show that despite the attention given in the letters to the contingent problems of the churches, Paul's thought nevertheless contains a center, without which according to him "the truth of the gospel" (Gal. 2:14, 15) would be distorted. In Part Two I will explicate more thoroughly the precise relationship between contingency and coherence in Paul's thought.

For this purpose I choose intentionally Galatians and Romans as typical examples. My choice of these letters is dictated by the fact that both in the history of exegesis and in the history of doctrine they have often been used to exhibit Paul's systematic doctrinal thought.

At first glance, Romans does not seem addressed to a concrete situation. Galatians, which was clearly written with particular circumstances in mind, has regularly been used by interpreters to undergird the so-called dogmatic structure of Romans. Certain parts of Galatians had to serve as a hermeneutical supplement to the central themes of Romans, although the more explicit and extensive character of Romans was of course acknowledged. In any case, both letters are similar in vocabulary and content; and both seem to elucidate the main theme of Paul's gospel, the so-called "center" of Paul's thought: justification by faith alone.

According to a long-standing hermeneutical method, obscure texts in Scripture are to be explained with the help of clearer texts. This harmonizing procedure, however, turns Paul's thought into an abstraction, so that the decisive mark of his theology is neglected, that is, his concern for the concrete circumstances of his churches. Thus the false impression arises that Galatians might just as well have been sent to Rome or Romans to Galatia. Indeed, it seems as if both writings have a similar composition and exhibit similar themes when we observe the analogous movement from justification by faith in the first chapters to sacramental participation in Christ and to ethical exhortation in the later chapters (Galatians 1–4; 5–6; Romans 1–4; 6–8; 12:1—15:13). Galatians and Romans, then, have often been so conflated that the specific historical occasion of each letter was ignored. Romans seems capable of drawing Galatians, its "helpmate," into its own timeless current. Consequently, the occasional nature of both letters has been neutralized.[1]

Therefore, it might seem a fruitless undertaking to select precisely Galatians and Romans among Paul's letters for an investigation of his contextual way of doing theology. If, however, the contingent particularity of the so-called "doctrinal" letters Galatians and Romans can be demonstrated, then the central intention of Paul's thought has been clarified.

PAUL'S OCCASIONAL LETTERS

It is clear that apart from Romans and its "companion," Galatians, the remaining five authentic letters of Paul (1 and 2 Corinthians; 1 Thessalonians; Philippians; and Philemon) yield a clear picture of the mutual interplay between coherence and contingency.

1. This is especially true for Galatians.

(*a*) The "Pauline school," which produced Colossians, Ephesians, and the Pastoral Epistles, encountered hermeneutical difficulties when it attempted to fit Paul's authentic letters into its picture of "the catholic Paul." It was the clear intention of this Pauline school to make Paul's theology universally relevant for the post-Pauline period. It tried as much as possible to suppress the contingent aspects of Paul's letters. Therefore, it is often difficult for New Testament scholars to determine the precise historical circumstances behind these letters. The post-Pauline letters, then, yield a picture that contradicts that of Paul's authentic letters. Whereas it is often difficult to determine the coherent center of the Pauline letters, the problem with the post-Pauline letters is exactly the reverse, that is, how to establish their contingency. Thus it becomes apparent that it was difficult for the post-Pauline period to preserve Paul's interplay of contingency and coherence.

(*b*) We have observed (chapter 2) that Paul's theological method consists in embodying the coherent center of the gospel in contingent, historical circumstances. For this reason, I really should have chosen the obviously contingent letters as primary examples for my thesis, rather than the so-called "systematic" letter to the Romans, which does not seem to be an occasional-contingent letter at all (see below, pp. 44–45).

These letters, especially 1 Corinthians with its question-answer style (e.g., 1 Corinthians 5:5-15; more specifically: 1 Cor. 7:1, 25; 8:1; 12:1; 15:12; 16:1), are in this respect more lucrative than Romans. However, if it can be shown that in the so-called doctrinal letters of Galatians and Romans Paul uses a method similar to that in his other letters, then one can claim that Paul's entire thought is based on a contextual way of thinking that focuses on the particular situations of his churches.

In that case, we would have to acknowledge that Paul's method is less concerned with "orthodoxy" than with "orthopraxis." This also means that Paul's contextual way of doing theology contrasts with our modern tendency of "purely cognitive thinking," according to which it ought to be possible to distill an inductive logic and a "timeless doctrinal system" from the pragmatically oriented thought of Paul.

In addition to 1 Corinthians, the contingent character of 2 Corinthians, 1 Thessalonians, Philippians, and Philemon is clear. Philemon is a personal letter that treats the problem of the possible manumission of Onesimus, a runaway slave. First Thessalonians is almost entirely an extended thanksgiving, while Philippians probably contains an early collection of fragments from several Pauline letters, although scholars have frequently made the mistake of portraying the Christ hymn in 2:5-11 as its theological center. Second Corinthians is as well an early collection of contingent writings.[2] Thus in view of the contingent character of Paul's letters and his contextual way of doing theology, it comes as no surprise that the postapostolic church not only authored "catholic" letters in the name of Paul but also elevated Romans, along with the more "ecumenical," universal portions of Galatians and 1 Corinthians, as the "principal letters" (*Hauptbriefe*).

In this connection, at least three key questions arise:

(*a*) How do we determine the abiding coherence in these contingent letters? For instance, should we not admit that 1 Thessalonians—whatever its "center" may be—represents "the early Paul"? Does not it then follow that the "later," more "mature" Paul reconsidered, changed, or even rejected his earlier teaching? And do we not also have to acknowledge that Paul surrenders the internal connection between the coherent center of the gospel and the contingent situations of the Corinthians when he makes the resurrection of the dead an inherent part of the center of the gospel and the necessary condition for their salvation (1 Corinthians 15)? Indeed, the Corinthians are Christians who regard—in the manner of Rudolf Bultmann and his school—the resurrection of the dead as an insignificant

2. Cf., for example, Günter Bornkamm, "Die Vorgeschichte," in *Gesammelte Aufsätze* 4:162-94.

Jewish notion that has little or nothing in common with the center of the gospel and moreover represents an unnecessary obstacle for Greek ears.

(*b*) Granted that we can determine the coherence of a specific letter, how does the specific coherence of a single letter relate to the overarching and universally valid coherence of all the other letters of Paul? Is there amid the situational contingency of the various letters really an overarching coherent unity, which is valid for all the letters? In other words, how are contingent diversity and coherent unity related? For instance, if 1 Thessalonians represents the convictions of an "early Paul" that he later abandoned, how can this letter be used to specify the abiding center of Paul's thought?

(*c*) And apart from these problems, is it possible to identify the coherence of literary documents with a definitive truth, that is, with "the truth of the gospel" (Gal. 2:4, 15)? It seems that the term "coherence" primarily means cohesiveness or consistency of thought, that is, the logical coherence of a text. However, in this context we should remember that according to Paul the Holy Spirit not only speaks coherently "with intelligible words" (1 Cor. 14:9) but also confers upon this coherent knowledge the power of the truth of the gospel.

The difficulty of detecting a coherent center in Paul's thought has misled many scholars to construct a flexible, evolving center, that is, an evolution scheme that traces the development from the "early" to the "mature" Paul. In this manner C. H. Dodd[3] and F. F. Bruce[4] have designated Ephesians as the climax of Paul's thought.

I want to maintain that the interplay between contingency and coherence is more appropriate for Paul's gospel than such an evolutionary model. In many cases this model only employs the contingent aspects of the letters in order

3. Dodd, *The Meaning of Paul for Today.*
4. Bruce, *Paul, Apostle of the Heart Set Free,* 424: "Ephesians represents the quintessence of Paul's thought."

to trace a theological process in Paul's psyche.[5] And thus
one risks the danger of disregarding the text of the letters
and thus failing to give the texts the serious consideration
they warrant (see chapter 1).

GALATIANS AND ROMANS

Thus far I have attempted to delineate the occasional and
contextual character of Paul's letters. Now I will show how
the so-called doctrinal letters to the Galatians and Romans
fit into this picture. Despite the hermeneutical parallels of
these letters, they must each be viewed in their particularity.
The strong polemical thrust of Galatians already points to
this. But even Romans is no *compendium doctrinae Chris-
tianae*,[6] although since the time of Philipp Melanchthon
this letter's systematic character often has been regarded as
obvious. Much time and energy was invested in exposing
the architectural structure of Romans, while its character
as a letter was often neglected. F. C. Baur's historical approach to the letter in the nineteenth century precipitated
a new wave of research.[7] But this venture was dropped
soon thereafter because it was deemed to be theologically
unproductive. Moreover, the rise of neo-orthodoxy re-
vived the view of the letter as "dogmatics in outline" or
as a literary treatise that represented in a unique manner
the center of Paul's thought.

It is a mistake, however, to consider Romans a timeless
theological treatise that contains the so-called essence of
Paul's theological thought. In this manner we misunder-
stand Paul's theological method, for in Romans he is not
composing a *summa theologica* or dealing with the "eternal
truth" of the gospel, or with a dogmatic monologue. His
purpose is apostolic-kerygmatic rather than dogmatic; for
him the gospel has the power to illuminate a historical
situation in the light of God's redemptive plan in Christ.

---

5. E.g., from Galatians via Corinthians to Romans; see Hübner, *Law in
Paul's Thought;* Drane, *Paul, Libertine or Legalist?;* Schnelle, "Der erste Thessalonicherbrief und die Entstehung der paulinischen Anthropologie."
    6. Melanchthon, "Römerbrief-Kommentar" (1532).
    7. Baur, *Paul, the Apostle of Jesus Christ,* 312-81.

I will now discuss the problem of particularity and universalism—that is, the relationship between contingency and coherence—with reference to two parallel themes in Galatians and Romans: *faith* (Galatians 3; Romans 4) and the *law* (Galatians 3; Romans 7). The individuality of both letters further requires an exposition of Paul's *eschatology* (see below, pp. 47–52). I will try to show that the particularity of situations not only compels Paul to construct a highly nuanced and differentiated argument, but also requires from him a variety of kerygmatic emphases.

Paul is often accused of inconsistent thinking or of showing a lack of sophistication.[8] But those who make such charges hardly ever question their own ideological presuppositions. They overlook the fact that Paul uses a method entirely different from the systematic and logical Western mode of thought that they often attribute to him. An empirical theology such as Paul's has its own characteristics that cannot be properly assessed in terms of abstract thought structures.[9] Instead, the essence of Paul's thought is determined by the particularity of Paul's argumentation and its kerygmatic focus. Therefore, Paul's specific hermeneutical method is no obstacle in defining the center of his theology. Rather, this method is simply the necessary entrance to his unique way of thinking.

Faith in Galatians 3 and Romans 4

Faith is a prominent theme in the Abraham story of Galatians 3 and Romans 4. The key text in both chapters is Gen. 15:6: "Abraham believed God, and it was reckoned to him as righteousness" (Gal. 3:6; Rom. 4:3). The difference in the movement of the argument between Galatians 3 and Romans 4 is not immediately apparent, because

8. See, e.g., Schoeps, *Paul,* 213: "Paul's fundamental misapprehension" of the law; Sanders, *Paul, the Law, and the Jewish People,* 144–48: "[Paul's] lack of systematic thinking about the law"; and Räisänen, "Paul's Theological Difficulties with the Law" in *The Torah and Christ,* 22: "Paul the theologian is a less coherent and less convincing thinker than is commonly assumed."

9. See, e.g., Belser, who characterizes Paul's thought as based on a dogmatic perspective (*Lehrstandpunkt*) in *Einleitung,* 509; and Philippi, who regards it as a "dogmatic exposition," *Commentar* 1:xx.

in both chapters Abraham is cast as the prototype of faith, a man who is justified by God on account of his faith and whose faith was fulfilled by Christ. Abraham functions as Paul's key figure in Scripture, the person of faith and the promise, realities that are prior to the coming of the law and are incompatible with it. Whereas the law is opposed to faith, faith is saving faith because it is a radical trust in the God of the promise and does not rely on human boasting or on the works of the law. As saving faith it breaks down the barrier between Jew and Gentile, because the Scripture foretold and demonstrated in Abraham its inclusive character (Gal. 3:8; Rom. 4:11). But this general interpretation of the Abraham story is inadequate because it abstracts from Paul's particular focus in each of the parallel chapters.

In Galatians 3 the key word is "promise" (*epangelia:* noun and verb forms appear nine times), while the verb "to reckon" (*logizomai:* ten times) dominates Romans 4. "Promise" also plays an important role in Romans 4 (five times), but it only appears in verses 13–22. The verb "to reckon," on the other hand, is absent from the discussion in Galatians, except for the citation of Gen. 15:6 in Gal. 3:6. In contrast to Romans, Paul's exegesis of Gen. 15:6 here does not focus on the verb "to reckon" (*logizomai*) but rather on "faith" (*episteusen* and *pistis,* vv. 6–14) and "promise" (vv. 14–22). Moreover, the pitch of the argument is quite different in Romans. In Romans 4 Abraham (4:5) is introduced in a context of boasting (4:2; cf. 3:27) and his status is depicted as that of a "godless one" (4:5). The focus is here on God's act of "reckoning" in the context of sin and boasting.

In fact, the terms "boasting," "godless," and "reckoning" do not occur in Galatians 3. Here the emphasis is not on that triangle, but on "faith," "Gentiles," and "works." Though the different use of vocabulary does not by itself constitute a sharp contrast with Romans, it nevertheless points to different nuances. In this context, we should especially notice the absence of Hab. 2:4 ("he who through faith is righteous shall live") from the discussion in Romans 4 and its very different position and significance in the argument of both letters (Rom. 1:17; Gal. 3:11). Habakkuk 2:4 constitutes the basic theme of the entire letter to the Romans (1:17) and provides the basis for its eschatological flow of thought in chapters 6–8 (cf. "shall live" [*zesetai*], Hab. 2:4b in 1:17b). In Galatians 3, to the contrary, Hab. 2:4 (Gal 3:11) has a subordinate place and serves only as a running commentary on Gen. 15:6 (Gal. 3:11).[10]

For Paul, as for contemporary Judaism, Hab. 2:4 and Gen. 15:6 are closely associated. In Judaism the texts provide proof that the Jews' faith-righteousness (Hab. 2:4) is founded on Abraham's relationship of trust in God (Gen. 15:6). It seems, therefore, as if both Galatians and Romans employ Hab. 2:4 to support the statement of Gen. 15:6. But behind the different uses of Hab. 2:4 and Gen. 15:6 in Galatians and Romans lies a different function of these texts. Whereas in Galatians 3 Gen. 15:6 is the key verse and Hab. 2:4 plays only a subordinate role (3:6, 11), in Romans Hab. 2:4 is the key verse for the entire letter, whereas Gen. 15:6 occupies a rather secondary place in the discussion (Rom. 1:17; 4:3). Again, whereas Hab. 2:4 is well suited to the topic of "faith" in Galatians 3, because this verse along with Gen. 15:6 highlights this theme, the emphasis on "reckoning" in Romans 4 renders any reference to Hab. 2:4 superfluous.[11] Therefore, it is striking in Rom. 1:17 and Gal. 3:11 that Hab. 2:4 is appropriated in such different ways: In Galatians the emphasis rests on "faith" in opposition to "doing," while in Romans the accent lies much more on God's unilateral gift of righteousness (Rom. 1:16).

We can say then that Romans 4 yields a more complex picture than Galatians 3 on the topic of faith: In Romans 4 faith can mean not only faith in the God of Christ (v. 24) but also faith in God's promise (vv. 13, 14, 16). To the

10. See Koch, *Die Schrift als Zeuge des Evangeliums,* 276 and 290. He overlooks the difference between Gal. 3:11 and Rom. 1:17.

11. See the stress on *logizesthai* in Rom. 4:1-11 (vv. 3, 4, 5, 6, 8 [Ps. 32:1], 9, 10, 11).

contrary, in Galatians 3 faith is directed exclusively toward its unique object, Christ, so that faith means "faith" in and "obedience" *to Christ* (vv. 5, 7, 9, 11, 12-14, 22, 23, 25, 26). However, in Romans 4 faith is characterized basically as trust, especially when Abraham's "trust" is contrasted with the "mistrust" (*apistia*) of humanity (v. 20).

The word "seed" (*sperma*) in Galatians 3 (vv. 16 [three times], 19, 26) refers exclusively to Christ (v. 16) and to Christians in "Christ" (vv. 18–24). In Romans 4, however, "seed" (4:13, 16, 18) refers to both the descendants of Abraham (v. 13), that is, to Jews, and Gentiles (vv. 16, 18). Abraham is here portrayed as "the father of many nations" (vv. 17, 18), that is, as the symbolic figure for the unity of Jews and Gentiles in the one Christian church,[12] whereas this idea does not occur in Galatians 3.

Furthermore, in Romans 4 Paul interprets Gen. 15:6 in the light of Gen. 15:5 ("so numerous shall your descendants be") (v. 18) and also draws Gen. 17:5 (vv. 17, 18) into the discussion, because here God calls Abram "Abraham" (*pater pollon ethnon*): "You shall no longer be called Abram. Your name shall be Abraham; for I have made you a father of many nations" (Gen. 17:5). Abraham's seed refers to a plurality of peoples and thus becomes the figure who unifies the peoples of Jews and Gentiles. To the contrary, in Galatians Christ alone is the seed, in whom all are one (Gal. 3:16, 20). Likewise, Christ alone is the content of the promise, because he is the exclusive seed of Abraham (v. 16).

In other words, the argument in Galatians 3 moves from Abraham to Christ, who is the fulfillment of the promise (v. 19b). As a result, the argument of Galatians 3 is christocentric, not only because Christ is the central object of faith but also because the chapter argues that faith was impossible before the coming of Christ. Abraham, then, represents here the "pre-gospel" (*proeuangelion,* v. 8); he is the figure of the promise that is only now realized in Christ (v. 25: "but now that faith has come").

12. See *propator* in vv. 1, 11, 12, 16, 17, 18.

Moreover, the discontinuity in salvation-history has a much sharper edge in Galatians than in Romans:

1. The promise and the Torah are antithetical principles, because the Torah is a later interloper into the history of salvation (Gal. 3:17).

2. The curse of the Torah makes Christ's sacrifice necessary (Gal. 3:13). Only because of Christ's death on the cross is "the curse" on humanity lifted, thus making it possible for "the blessing" to Abraham once again to flow to the Gentiles (3:10-14). Thus, Gen. 15:6 is interpreted more in terms of the promise of faith than of its actuality, because the reality of faith is possible only in Christ and was not really available prior to his coming.

The salvation-historical discontinuity of Galatians 3, with its christocentric scope and its antithesis to the Torah, is much less apparent in Romans 4. Here the continuity of salvation-history and the continuous reality of faith in both the pre-Christian and the Christian period are stressed. The inherent quality of faith as trust and obedience seems here to overshadow the importance of Christ, who in Galatians is the sole object and sole possibility of faith. Whereas Galatians 3 presents Christ as the only object of faith and Abraham as the symbol of the promise, in Romans 4 the object of faith is the God of Abraham, who is the same as the God of the Christians, that is, the one who justifies the ungodly, just as he justified Abraham (v. 5) and the one who raises the dead (v. 17), just as he raised up new seed for Abraham's "dead body" (v. 19). In other words, in Romans 4 *God* is the one who reckons righteousness to faith alone (vv. 3, 23).

The Old Testament faith of Abraham and Christian faith are here merged to such an extent that the explicit, christological focus of faith appears only at the very end of the chapter (vv. 24–25). The structural analogy between the Old Testament faith of Abraham and Christian faith, then, is more apparent in Romans 4 than in the promise-fulfillment scheme of Galatians 3. Thus we see that the shift away from the christocentric emphasis in Galatians 3 to the theocentric argument in Romans 4 serves the continuous thrust of the salvation-historical argument of Romans 4.

Moreover, the person of Abraham is much more central in Romans than in Galatians. In contrast to the narrative of Galatians 3, Rom. 4:17-21 gives, as it were, a psychological sketch of Abraham's faith and describes how faith operates amid the trials of the world.

In addition, there are significant differences with respect to the character of the "promise": In Galatians 3 the promise given to Abraham is fulfilled in Christ (3:22) and in the gift of the Spirit (3:14). According to Paul, Christians—unlike Old Testament believers—do not *hope* in "the *promise*," but rather they *hope* in the "glory of God"—a thought that is also illustrated by the transition from the term "promise" (Rom. 4:16-21) to the "glory of God" (Rom. 5:1-2). Galatians 3:22 then represents both the general teaching of early Christianity and that of Paul (cf. also Rom. 15:8; 2 Cor. 1:20). In Romans 4, however, Paul appears to abandon this basic distinction between the hope in the *promise* of the Old Testament and the new Christian accent on the "hope of glory." In Rom. 4:20 the *promise* seems to remain the abiding object of faith, for it characterizes Abraham's faith as an example for Christians. In fact, both in Romans 4 and in Hebrews 11 the Old Testament promise is fused with the specific object of Christian hope.

By way of summary, it can be said that although both Romans 4 and Galatians 3 are dealing with salvation-history, they interpret it quite differently. Galatians 3 focuses on the fundamental principles of salvation-history, whereas Romans 4 centers on the existential stance of Abraham's personal faith as an example for all believers.

Galatians 3 almost presents us with a "realized eschatology," since the fullness of eschatological reality coincides with the Christ-event. In fact, the word group "hope" hardly enters into the discussion in Galatians (*elpizō* is entirely absent; *elpis* occurs only in Gal. 5.5). In Romans, however, the future-eschatological thrust of Paul's argument is much more prominent (cf. Romans 5–8). Faith in the promise characterizes not only Abraham but also the Christian believer (4:20-25) while "promise" and "hope" seem to be used synonymously (5:1-5).

In Galatians 3 Paul polemicizes against Judaizers by arguing for a sharp christological discontinuity in salvation-history, while in Romans 4 he allows for the continuity of salvation-history. Here Paul emphasizes Abraham as a paradigm of faith for Jews and Gentiles alike (v. 12). To be sure, Rom. 4:14-16, which also opposes true faith to the law, has a thrust that reminds one of Galatians. But these verses are polemical asides and do not present the main theme of the chapter. Although Paul challenges the Jew to become a "true" Jew like Abraham, this does not mean that Judaism is "demonized," as this threatens to occur in Galatians 3.

It is clear that Paul addresses very different situations in Romans 4 and Galatians 3. Whereas Romans 4 develops the thesis of Rom. 3:29-31,[13] Galatians 3 explicates the faith-law antithesis of Gal. 3:2-5.

Furthermore, notice that Romans introduces not only Abraham but also Adam into its argument, whereas the Adam story is absent from Galatians. In Romans the figures of Abraham and Adam complement each another (Romans 4 and 5:12-21). Abraham typifies the continuity of the history of salvation, while Adam typifies the dualistic, apocalyptic theology of the two ages. The focus of the Abraham story is the relation of Jew and Gentile and stresses God's enduring faithfulness to his plan of redemption. Christ functions here to confirm the stance of faith that Abraham has already exhibited and that applies to all "who walk in his footsteps," both the circumcised and the uncircumcised (Rom. 4:12; cf. vv. 24–25).

The Adam typology in Rom. 5:12-21, to the contrary, does not emphasize continuity but rather discontinuity.

---

13. God justifies both Jews and Gentiles (v. 30); "we establish the law" (v. 31b).

Here the last (eschatological) Adam reverses radically what the first Adam has initiated in world history: sin and death (cf. also 1 Cor. 15:20-22). The dualistic, apocalyptic thrust of the Adam typology underscores the radical newness of God's act in Christ. Thus, the Adam typology centers on the ontological antithesis of death and life, whereas the Abraham story in Romans 4 underlines the continuity of faith within the history of salvation.

In the Adam typology, the death of Christ functions as the negation of the old world's values and as the transference of believers into a resurrection mode of existence. Christ is here the inaugurator of the new eschatological world of "life" (Rom. 5:17, 18, 21) and the initiator of the "new creation" (cf. Gal. 6:15; 2 Cor. 5:17). Within this apocalyptic Adam typology there is no room for a figure like Abraham, who already, according to Romans 4, constitutes within the old age the seed or reality of the new age to come. Adam and Abraham cannot be integrated easily into a "systematic" view of history, because both figures operate on different tracks and levels of salvation-history in Paul's thought. In Rom. 5:12-21 the Adam story, indeed, transcends "the Jewish question" of the social relationship between Jew and Gentile, despite the prominence of this issue in Romans 1–4. Thus we see that Paul raises his argument to a new level in Rom. 5:12-21, where he points out that the social barrier between Jew and Gentile is not the ultimate human problem. Rather, the ultimate division in humankind is not between Jew and Greek, but between being "in Adam" or "in Christ." In the light of the redemptive reversal of the human condition in "the last Adam," Christ, all other distinctions fall away. According to Paul, then, Christ is not a "new Abraham" or a "new Moses," but the new eschatological "last" Adam.

Whereas Christ in Romans 4 confirms and fulfills the faith of Abraham, according to Rom. 5:12-21 he, as the new Adam, radically reverses the disastrous ontological and cosmic consequences of Adam's disobedience, because in Christ's obedience the "new man" and the "new creation" are reconstituted. Along these lines Paul can confirm both the continuity between the old and new dispensations (chap. 4) and the discontinuity of the new dispensation (5:12-21).[14]

The Abraham story in Galatians 3 has quite a different focus. Here the hermeneutical key is the discontinuity of salvation-history. The new age of faith can be realized only in Christ (3:22, 23, 25), while the old age is exclusively characterized by bondage to sin (v. 22). Here Abraham is not so much cast as the actualizer of faith but as the recipient of the promise, and hence represents the "pre-gospel" (*proeuangelion*) (v. 8; cf. vv. 15–18). The apocalyptic motif of discontinuity dominates the Abraham story in Galatians because the promise to Abraham—fulfilled by Christ, his exclusive seed—is here sharply contrasted with the law and its curse. The divergent use of the Abrahamic figure in Galatians and Romans is to be explained by the different contingent situations addressed by both letters. The different *Sitz im Leben* of both communities forces Paul to accentuate different aspects of the argument.

In Galatians 3 Paul attacks Judaizers, who fuse their ancestor Abraham with the Torah and with Christ. Here he casts the Abraham story in an utterly discontinuous way. The Judaizers in Galatia have exchanged "the truth of the gospel" (Gal. 2:6, 14) for their counter-gospel. Thus Paul must safeguard the *solus Christus* and the *sola fide* of his gospel against the Judaizing synthesis of law and gospel. Romans, on the other hand, is addressed to a church whose unity is being threatened by schism (chaps. 14 and 15). More specifically, the threat stems from sectarian tendencies (chaps. 14 and 15; cf. also 1:18—4:25; 11:18-25; 12:3), which threaten Paul's future missionary activity, because Paul needs the support of the church at Rome for his mission to Spain.

The comparison between Galatians and Romans leaves us with this question: If the various sociological circumstances of the churches determine to such a large extent

---

14. See also 2 Cor. 3:4-11, where both continuity and discontinuity between the old and new dispensations (*diakonia*) are emphasized.

the content of Paul's proclamation of the gospel, how then can we speak of a unified coherence of Paul's gospel that encompasses *all* his authentic letters? This question is all the more urgent because it seems that the contingent circumstances of the churches have left an important mark on Paul's dialogue with his hearers and thus on the coherence of his gospel.

The Law in Galatians 3 and Romans 7

Galatians was written in the midst of a crisis situation that demanded radical decisions. The Judaizers' synthesis of Abraham, promise, Torah, and Christ required a firm refutation. Thus the Torah and Christ are presented as antithetical principles, so that the confession of Christ excludes the Torah and circumcision.

The contingency of Romans yields a very different picture: Paul is here engaged in a dialogue with Jews and gentile Christians not only about his stance toward the law and Judaism, but also about the question of God's faithfulness toward Israel. His statements are directed to former God-fearers and Jews who, according to Paul, have not sufficiently recognized the radical nature of God's act in Christ. Paul attempts to clarify that only God's work in Christ can deliver them from the Torah's sentence of death and from the powers of sin, the flesh, and death. Whereas Paul's argument in Galatians is primarily polemic, he tries in Romans to win his addressees over to his position. The language of Galatians, unlike that of Romans, is sarcastic and aggressive, the mode of argumentation is subversive, fragmentary, and occasionally ambivalent and unclear. This polemical style results, therefore, in a loss of systematic order.

Although Romans 7 makes statements about the Torah that are even more radical than those in Galatians, the context is different, as a comparison of the "apologies" of the law in Rom. 7:7-13 and Gal. 3:19-20 makes clear.

The argument in Gal. 3:19-20 is cryptic and carries a negative thrust, which even denies the divine origin of the law (v. 20). The passage is preceded by a defamation of the law, because the law is here equated with a "curse" that is opposed to the promise to Abraham and its blessing (3:10-18). The law not only cursed Christ "on the tree" (v. 13), but it is also portrayed as an intruder that splits salvation-history apart and illegitimately inserts itself between the promise to Abraham and the Christ-event. Paul bases this accusation on Scripture itself (Hab. 2:4 *contra* Lev. 18:5; cf. Gal. 3:11, 12), for, according to his conviction, the law has no inherent connection with the "testament" (*diatheke*) of the promise (Gal. 3:15). The law then has a negative ontological dimension (3:19b, 20). Moreover, when Paul attempts to give an "apology of the law" (3:19-22), his argument is rather cryptic and hard to understand. Paul seems so agitated here that he posits statements (e.g., vv. 19, 21) without sufficient warrant or explication.

Romans, however, contains a full apology of the law in Rom. 7:7-13 that spills over into vv. 14–25. This section serves to put Paul's radical and shocking anti-Jewish thesis of 7:5 in its proper light: "While we were living in the flesh, our sinful passions, aroused by the law, were at work in our members to bear fruit for death." The apology in Romans succeeds because Paul here not only gives a positive ontology of the law, but also makes important distinctions between the law's ontological and ontic functions—something Galatians does not do.

Where in Galatians 3 do we find statements like "The law is holy, and the commandment is holy and just and good" (Rom. 7:12) or "the law is spiritual" (Rom. 7:14)? Moreover, where in Galatians do we hear, "Do we then overthrow the law by this faith? By no means! On the contrary, we uphold the law" (Rom. 3:31). Instead, Galatians offers only a negative counterpart: "Is the law then against the promises of God? Certainly not!" (Gal. 3:21). Paul's claim that for believers "the just requirement of the law is fulfilled" (Rom. 8:4, *plerothe*) is only hinted at in Gal. 5:23 (but cf. 5:14). The idea that the giving of the Torah is one of Israel's privileges (Rom. 9:4) and that there is an "advantage" to being a Jew, in that the Jews "have been entrusted with the oracles of God," (Rom. 3:1-2) does not fit the argument of Galatians. The issue of a "third use" of the law for Christians can be discussed only on the basis of Romans, for Galatians offers no solid support for it.

Although Paul claims in Galatians that Christians "fulfill the law of Christ" (Gal. 6:2) and that "the whole law is fulfilled in one word" (5:14), that is, in the word of the Old Testament love commandment in Lev. 19:18, the precise nature of the Torah's relationship to the "law of Christ" remains unclear. Given the negative statements concerning the law in Galatians, the positive portrayal of "the Jewish problem" by Paul in Romans comes as a surprise. The difference Paul makes in Romans 7 between the positive ontology of the law and its negative, anthropological function allows him to draw a distinction between the law's divine origin and its abuse in the human situation by the power of sin—a distinction that enables him to emphasize the positive function of the law. The law unmasks not only the power of sin (Rom. 7:13; cf. Gal. 3:19) but also reveals to Christians the will of God (Rom. 8:4, 7). The relation between law and gospel is therefore construed differently in Romans and Galatians. In Galatians the law-gospel antithesis is central to the discussion; the law and Christ come into conflict "on the tree" of the cross (Gal. 3:13), where the law curses Christ. Although there is in Romans a similar collision between the promise, Christ, and the law (Rom. 4:13, 14; 7:5-6; 8:1-3), the scope of Paul's argument is directed elsewhere. Paul stresses indeed the inability of the law to save humanity (Rom. 8:3), but refrains from speaking about its curse (cf. Gal. 3:10-13). Likewise, in Romans Christ does not "abolish" the law as in Gal. 3:13 but rather fulfills the law's intent (Rom. 8:4; cf. 9:31). To be sure, both letters represent Christ as "the end of the law" (Rom. 10:4; Gal. 2:19-21; 5:4) and emphasize a salvation-historical dualism (Rom. 4:13-14; 7:4-6; Gal. 3:15-29). Nevertheless, Romans modifies the antithesis between the law and the gospel because the positive ontology of the law permits

Paul to incorporate its divine intent into the gospel. There-fore, although Christ is "the end of the law" (Rom. 10:4), he also fulfills its intent (Rom. 3:31; 8:3, 4, 7; cf. also 9:31; 10:4).

The apology of the law (Rom. 7:7-13) actually flows into a discussion of the human plight under the law (vv. 14–25). In the course of the argument Paul develops an anthropology that in an autobiographical manner depicts the internal conflict of the old Adam under the law. Because the law expresses the will of God and because "my inmost self" (v. 22) and "the law of my mind" (v. 23) consent to the law, the experience of sin's power as constitutive of my being (v. 14) is all the more desperate: Sin controls my innermost being by paralyzing my will and by deceiving me (v. 11) through the law. Nevertheless, the law is not demonic in and of itself, although it is misused by sin for demonic purposes. Indeed, it does incite me to sin and hence condemns and kills me. At the same time, the law uncovers the power of sin within me as my principal enemy.

In the final analysis, the law becomes my enemy because it confronts me with who I am: a person who "covets" (Rom. 7:7). Moreover, in Romans Paul develops a specific anthropology in the context of his discussion of the law (7:7-25). Paul's clarity here contrasts sharply with Gala-tians, where no specific anthropology emerges (in chap. 3) and where there is only a cryptic parallel (5:13-24) to his discussion in Romans 7.

The anthropological, subjective dimension of the law is much more apparent in Romans than in Paul's salvation-historical and ontological treatment of the law in Galatians. Whereas in Galatians the law functions to seal our sin before God (whether or not we are aware of it), in Romans the existential element is clear. Here the issue of "my own righteousness" (*idia dikaiosynē,* Rom. 10:3) surfaces—an issue absent in Galatians. Hence the importance of the theme of "boasting" in Romans (2:17, 23; 3:27; 4:2; 11:18), which is only a peripheral topic in Galatians (6:13; cf.

6:4, 14). Moreover, Romans shows that the experience of sin brought about by the law (Rom. 3:20; 7:7-13) is not simply something that only Christian hindsight brings about, as if its experience is unknown to the pre-Christian Jew.[15]

In contrast to Paul's claim in Phil. 3:6, that he was "as to zeal a persecutor of the church, as to righteousness under the law blameless," Romans at least suggests that faith in Christ answers on some level the Jew's awareness of sin that derives from an encounter with the law.[16]

Romans then is a dialogue with former Gentiles and Jews concerning "the Jewish question." Therefore, this question necessitates an argument that differs from the one mounted against the Judaizing problem in Galatia. Paul argues in Romans the function of the law within the context of the faithfulness and impartiality of God in salvation-history (Rom. 3:3; 9:6, 14) and emphasizes the privileged position of the Jews in the gospel (1:16; 2:9-10; cf. 11:11-29). In this context an apology of the law becomes important. Although Christ is "the end of the law" (10:4), the law served as the necessary negative counterpart (4:13; 5:13; 7:13) for the positive righteousness of God in Christ (3:21; 10:4). Romans and Galatians agree on this point. Yet the particular occasion of Paul's letter to the Galatians did not require an extensive apology of the law.[17] In Romans, however, the law and the Christ-event are not, as it were, equivalent ontological counterparts; they have become so only because of the depth of the human fall. In this way the Marcionite tendencies of Galatians are overcome in Romans not in the least because of the different contingencies and argumentations in both letters. Thus Romans clearly reinforces the function of the law as "custodian" (cf. also Gal. 3:24). It functions as such not only from the perspective of Christian hindsight into the history of salvation (Gal. 3:22-25) but already in the pre-Christian era when the law ruled over us (Rom. 2:1-29).

15. Thus, for example, Paul's appeal in Rom. 2:1-29 to the Jewish experience of sin.
16. Cf. Luther's *deuterus usus legis* (second use of the law).
17. An apology is only hinted at in Gal. 3:19-21.

The differing emphases of Paul's interpretation of the law in Romans and Galatians may well have affected the discussion of the law in the history of Christian doctrine. Edward A. Dowey observes, "For Luther the chief connotation of law is self-justification and condemnation, whereas for Calvin it is the structure of love."[18]

And so our discussion of faith and the law in Galatians and Romans has pointed to the contextual manner of Paul's argumentation. But the discussion also leaves us with an important question: Do we have to conclude that because Paul's theology is so decisively determined by contingent situations, a search for a coherent center of his thought is futile? Or will it be possible to detect in and behind Paul's contingent arguments the presence of such a center? A satisfactory answer to this question will depend on a more precise explication of the relation between contingency and coherence in Paul's thought.

18. E. A. Dowey in personal communication.

4

The Coherence of
the Gospel

We may now ask whether a coherence or normative "center" can be discerned in Paul's theology given the overall contextual nature of his letters. This question takes on added significance in light of my twofold thesis that (a) the apocalyptic motif forms the foundation of his thought and that (b), more specifically, the apocalyptic triumph of God constitutes its focal point.

OBJECTIONS TO APOCALYPTIC

One could raise the objection that these are rather arbitrary hypotheses. Why should apocalyptic and especially the triumph of God be given more importance than one of the various contingent structures of Paul's thought? In short, why not simply admit that Paul's theology is thoroughly contingent, as many New Testament scholars maintain?[1]

The issue of the coherence of Paul's theology is also important because ever since the Enlightenment scholars have drawn a distinction between a "profound" and "coherent" Jesus and an "opportunistic" Paul. In this way Paul is often regarded as a radical anti-Semite or as a regressive

1. Cf., e.g., Räisänen, Sanders with qualifications, Drane, Hübner, and Schoeps.

Jewish thinker, who perverted the message of Jesus.[2] Thus
Friedrich Nietzsche characterized Paul as follows: "He is
the first Christian, the true founder of Christianity! Until
him there were only a few Jewish sectarians."[3]

Although such views did not gain lasting influence, some
scholars deemed it necessary to reclaim Paul by attributing
to him a keen intuition, which he was, however, unable
to formulate adequately.[4] Others argued in a similar fashion
that Paul was not able to translate his "basic convictions"
into logically convincing theological language.[5]

Along with Reformed theology, I claim, however, that
Paul's theology actually exhibits a specific "center." But
this center should be viewed as a much more flexible phenomenon than many systematic theologians and New Testament scholars have thus far proposed. I have already
argued above (see chapter 2) that it is a mistake to conceive
the center of Paul's theology too narrowly or to define it
in overly general and abstract terms. By "too narrowly"
I mean the use of fossilized terminology such as "justification through faith"[6] or "sacramental participation and
oneness with Christ."[7] On the other hand, the words "general" and "abstract" refer to phrases like "being in Christ"[8]
or "the lordship of Christ."[9] For this reason I prefer the
flexible term "coherence" to the rigid term "center" or
"core." Moreover, I claim that an apocalyptic substratum
or background constitutes the "coherence" of Paul's gospel.
This coherence is determined by Paul's apocalyptic interpretation of the Christ-event and culminates in God's triumph over all the powers that are opposed to his rightful
lordship over the creation.

2. So, e.g., Friedrich Nietzsche, Ernest Renan, and Paul Anton de Lagarde.
3. Nietzsche, "The First Christian," in *The Dawn of Day*, no. 68.
4. Räisänen, *Paul and the Law*, 262–69.
5. Sanders, *Paul, the Law, and the Jewish People*, 44, 147; and Patte, *Paul's Faith and the Power of the Gospel*.
6. Wendland, *Die Mitte der paulinischen Botschaft*; Käsemann, " 'The Righteousness of God' in Paul," in *New Testament Questions of Today*, 168–82.
7. Thus, e.g., Schneider, *Die Passionsmystik des Paulus*; Cerfaux, *The Spiritual Journey of Saint Paul*; Wikenhauser, *Pauline Mysticism*.
8. Whiteley, *The Theology of Saint Paul*, xiv, 45; Deissmann, *Paul*.
9. Davies, *Paul and Rabbinic Judaism*, 177, 86-110.

The coherent center of Paul's gospel reflects then a symbolic structure, that is, a newly ordered field of apocalyptic metaphors that come to concrete expression in the different contingent situations of the churches. Paul's theology is constituted by a necessary interplay between coherence and contingency. We can better understand the specific character of Paul's hermeneutic when we compare it not only with Jewish but also with subsequent Christian hermeneutics. These hermeneutical methods frequently have had a rigid and casuistic character in comparison with the more fluid, spontaneous, and prophetic manner of Paul's thought. This contrast is especially noticeable when compared with Jewish halakic interpretations of the law and with the fixed declarations of the Christian confessions of faith in later Christian sources.[10] Thus the term "coherence" indicates that the center of Paul's theology is not marked by a closed, rigid doctrinal system. "Coherence" resembles more the Olympic logo, in which the various circles are held together by a common bond.

The apocalyptic aspects of Paul's thought, therefore, do not simply represent a series of isolated contingent statements; rather, they determine the whole field of Paul's contextual assertions. Paul's apocalyptic scheme of thought provides the filter for the coherent expression of "the truth of the gospel." As Ephesians formulates it in a Pauline manner: "We should no longer be children, tossed to and fro and carried about by every wind of doctrine, by the deception and craftiness of men, which leads astray" (Eph. 4:14). "Tossed to and fro by every wind of doctrine" would mean for Paul the loss of coherence and a surrender to a diffuse contingency, that is, to an opportunistic misinterpretation of the gospel. Such a position would undermine any basic relation to the coherence of the gospel.

Finally, I would argue that the issue of Paul's apocalyptic can only be addressed properly if the distinction between apocalyptic *genre,* apocalyptic *movements,* and apocalyptic

---

10. Thus, for example, "the entrusted deposit of truth" (*parathēkē*) in 1 Tim. 6:20.

motifs is upheld. Consequently, the fact that only a few passages in Paul are "purely" apocalyptic, as Jörg Baumgarten and Leander Keck have shown,[11] does not affect my claim about Paul's apocalyptic thought. To be sure, the characteristic language of apocalyptic, such as "this present" and "the coming age," "the kingdom of God" and "the day of the Lord," rarely surfaces in Paul's letters. Nevertheless, Paul's churches were apocalyptic movements, and Paul's theology cannot be grasped without taking note of the numerous apocalyptic motifs that underlie his thought. I have elaborated this thesis in greater detail in my book on Paul.[12] It must be examined anew, however, in the light of two important criticisms: (1) In *Paul the Apostle* I dealt with the morphology of apocalyptic in a brief and abstract manner. (2) I obscured and blurred the necessary distinction between the apocalyptic background of Paul's thought and its contingent expression in specific situations.

Here is my response to these criticisms: (1) In my portrayal of apocalyptic I followed the definitions proposed by Philipp Vielhauer and Klaus Koch,[13] that is, their delineations of the three essential elements of apocalyptic: historical dualism, universalism, and imminent expectation (see above, chapter 2). Although these elements represent necessary heuristic models, I neglected perhaps the most important aspect of biblical apocalyptic: the faithfulness and trustworthiness of God. This feature not only encompasses all the others but modifies them as well. Similarly, I neglected to describe the sociological structure of the various bearers of Jewish apocalyptic. It would have been helpful to provide a more thorough account of the groups and communities that espoused an apocalyptic religiosity.

(2) Ralph P. Martin has rightly criticized my blurring of the apocalyptic background with its contingent expression: "Apocalyptic itself of all the suggestions for a Pauline center

11. Baumgarten, *Paulus und die Apokalyptik;* Keck, "Paul and Apocalyptic Theology."
12. Beker, *Paul the Apostle.*
13. Vielhauer, "Introduction" in Hennecke-Schneemelcher, eds., *New Testament Apocrypha* 2:581–607; Koch, *The Rediscovery of Apocalyptic.*

is symbolic, and we are at a loss to know what is the rationale by which one symbol should be preferred above others, and indeed regarded as the basic premise explaining all the others."[14] This blending of the groundwork and its practical outworking in Paul's apocalyptic thought opened my presentation to further misinterpretations. Thus J. Louis Martyn remarked that I unjustifiably excluded Galatians from the coherent center of Paul's theology.[15] I had indeed argued that Paul did not stress "the coherent theme" of the triumph of God in Galatians because of the contingent crisis in Galatia. This thesis, however, is no longer tenable. How indeed could the apocalyptic theme of the gospel be said to go unmentioned in a letter where Paul emphasizes that "the truth of the gospel" is a matter of "revelation" (apokalypsis; cf. Gal. 1:12, 16; 2:2, 5, 14).

These critical observations necessitate a new inquiry into the coherent scheme of Paul's gospel. This pertains not only to the relationship of the gospel to its apocalyptic background, but also to the gospel's interplay with its inherently contingent reality. Therefore I will discuss these themes in what follows:

- Apocalyptic and the resurrection of Christ
- The cross of Christ and the demonic powers
- Christian life and the church: the appropriation and practice of the gospel in the horizon of hope

APOCALYPTIC AND THE RESURRECTION OF CHRIST

The apocalyptic interpretation of the Christ-event constitutes the coherent center of Paul's gospel. Already in 1917 William Morgan observed that "Paul's outlook is at bottom that of Jewish apocalyptic. While conceptions from other sources . . . have to be taken in account, they are superimposed on an apocalyptic groundwork."[16]

14. Ralph P. Martin, review of Paul the Apostle, J. Christiaan Beker, JBL 101 (1982):464.
15. J. Louis Martyn, review of Paul the Apostle, J. Christiaan Beker, Word and World 2 (1982):194–98.
16. Morgan, The Religion and Theology of Paul, 6; cf. also Kabisch, Die Eschatologie des Paulus (1893); Weiss, Jesus' Proclamation of the Kingdom of God (1900).

Jewish apocalyptic constitutes the substratum and master symbolism of Paul's thought for two reasons: (1) it constituted the language world of Paul the Pharisee and therefore (2) forms the indispensable filter, context, and grammar by which Paul appropriated and interpreted the Christ-event, that is, the *apokalypsis Iesou Christou* (Gal. 1:12; cf. 1:16; 2:2). The interplay between coherence and contingency is evident not only in the private experience of Paul's call, but also in the communal-apostolic activity of Paul's missionary mandate. The co-incidence of "conversion" and apostolic call in the Damascus experience (Gal. 1:15) demonstrates the twofold aspect of "the truth of the gospel": The apocalyptic interpretation of the cross and resurrection of Christ is the abiding solution not only to Paul's private contingency (in answering the crisis of his personal life), but also to the various problems of his churches (in answering their several crises).

It is clear that for Paul the resurrection of Christ stimulated rather than relaxed his longing for the parousia. Thus at the end of the theological exposition of Romans he writes: "Now may the God of hope fill you with all joy and peace in believing, so that you abound in hope in the power of the Holy Spirit" (Rom. 15:13). Likewise he stresses in Rom. 13:11: "Besides this you know what hour it is, how it is full time now for you to wake from sleep. For salvation is nearer to us now than when we first believed." And in 1 Thess. 1:9-10 he says, "For they themselves report concerning us what a welcome we had among you, and how you turned to God from idols, to serve a living and true God, and to wait for his Son from heaven, whom he raised from the dead, Jesus, who delivers us from the wrath to come."

Resurrection language is eschatological language that is intelligible only within an apocalyptic world of thought where it is at home. This language is about the world to come and thus constitutes an essential component of apocalyptic's expectation of the transformation and restoration of the whole cosmos. For this reason the resurrection of

Christ, the coming reign of God, and the resurrection of the dead belong inseparably together. The new creation in Christ (*kainē krisis;* cf. 2 Cor. 5:17 and Gal. 6:15) is an anticipation of the resurrection of the dead and a new creative act of God, "who gives life to the dead, and calls into existence the things that do not exist" (Rom. 4:17). "Resurrection," then, is more than a "noetic" notion as if resurrection is to be understood as a pure language—or kerygmatic event. It also has a clearly historical and on-tological referent, since it encompasses the transformation of the entire created order. Therefore, the resurrection of Christ does not simply mean a heavenly "rapture" (Enoch, Elijah), "ascension" or "rebirth" (as in the mystery relig-ions). Paul does not view the ascension of Jesus in terms of a "removal scene," as if a Gnostic redeemer leaves the world of corrupt matter, while he—leaving his body on the cross—returns to his spiritual abode in heaven, where pure Spirit unites itself with pure Spirit. Nor docs he view the resurrection in terms of a historical "reunion scene," as if Jesus returns to the flesh and resumes his previous companionship with his disciples, such as eating and talk-ing with them (Luke 24). We must not forget that in Paul the empty tomb tradition does not play any role; ". . . and that he was buried" (*etaphē,* 1 Cor. 15:4) simply underlines the reality of Christ's death. The resurrection of Christ means primarily the "bodily exaltation of Christ by God and his heavenly enthronement as Lord (Phil. 2:11). It signifies the exaltation of the crucified one, that is, it means the anticipation of the final apocalyptic resurrection of the dead and hence foreshadows the transformation of the cos-mos and the new form of resurrection life in the body.

Thus "resurrection" is a historical-ontological category, which since Christ's resurrection heralds in this world the dawn of a new age and the transformation of all things. Consequently, the God "who gives life to the dead" (Rom. 4:17; 2 Cor. 1:9) is not so much the God who works arbitrary miracles but rather the God who since the res-urrection of Christ has ushered in the world of the new age. He is, after all, the creator-redeemer, who "calls into existence the things that do not exist" (Rom. 4:17). Thus resurrection language expresses the presence of the new age in the midst of the old. And so Paul emphasizes a resurrection of the body but not of the flesh. For a resurrection of the flesh would distort Paul's apocalyptic thought, since it would underscore the continuity between the old age and the new age to such a degree that the spiritual transformation of the new age would be ignored.

The final resurrection will result in a complete apocalyptic renewal: "the new world" (*palingenesia*, Matt. 19:28; *1 Clem.* 9:4; cf. Mark 12:23: "In the resurrection whose wife will she be?"). In this way Paul speaks about Israel's conversion in the eschatological age as "life from the dead" (Rom. 11:15). Because resurrection is an apocalyptic category, Christ's resurrection can be understood only in an apocalyptic sense, that is, as a proleptic anticipation of the general resurrection in the coming age. Therefore, Paul presents the risen Christ as "the first fruits among those who have fallen asleep" (1 Cor. 15:20) or as "the firstborn among many brethren" (Rom. 8:29; cf. Col. 1:16). Thus the resurrection of Christ announces the final resurrection of the dead.

We must be aware of the fact that resurrection language cannot be understood if it is divorced from this temporal and cosmological framework. There is a necessary interrelationship between the resurrection of Christ and the new age to come. If we divorce these two events, for instance, by displacing the age to come to some distant point in time, or if we sever the event of Christ's resurrection from the general resurrection of the dead by dismissing the new age as a "myth," then a severe distortion occurs. For then Paul's resurrection language is compelled to function in a different semantic system, where it loses its intended meaning.

Paul combats this last point of view in 1 Corinthians 15. For, as Hellenistic Christians, the Corinthians are convinced that there is no need for a necessary relation between the resurrection of Christ and the coming new age.

The Context of 1 Corinthians 15

Before we pursue Paul's argument in 1 Corinthians 15, we must first consider the place of this chapter within the context of 1 Corinthians. This letter especially demonstrates the intimate relationship between contingency and coherence in Paul's thought, because it seems to consist of a series of contingent arguments. Contingency is apparent not only in the multiple problems and questions to which Paul must respond but also in the basic shift of the argument in the opening and closing chapters (chaps. 1–2 and 15). Whereas the main theme in the letter's early chapters (1 and 2) is the death of Christ, it is not the death of Christ but his resurrection that is the central issue in chapter 15. Thus it seems as if Paul has divorced Christ's death and resurrection in 1 Corinthians, because the absence of the resurrection theme in chapters 1 and 2 is just as striking as the almost complete absence of Christ's death in chapter 15.

In 1 Corinthians Paul addresses a variety of problems through a series of questions and answers: a case of incest, judicial matters, questions about worship, gnosis, marriage, church unity, spiritual gifts, and instructions concerning the collection for the saints. Where is unity to be found in the midst of this great variety of questions and problems? What constitutes "the canon within the canon" of this letter? Karl Barth attempted to show that the basic coherent theme of the letter must be located in the resurrection chapter (chap. 15), which connects all the contingent themes and at the same time forms the climax of the letter.[17] According to this view, Paul's argument about the resurrection of the dead is not to be considered as an ad hoc polemical or pastoral concern but rather as the hidden key to the whole letter. Barth's thesis is, in fact, substantiated by the thanksgiving (1 Cor. 1:4-9), because it summarizes the content of the letter and, above all, emphasizes the "waiting for the revealing [*tēn apokalypsin*] of our Lord Jesus Christ" (1:7) and "his sustenance to the

17. Barth, *The Resurrection of the Dead*, 13–124.

end" (1:8). This theme is subsequently developed in chapter 15.

The Theology of the Corinthians

The Corinthians do not live in an apocalyptic thought world; they live in the world of Hellenistic cosmology that thinks more in spatial-vertical categories than in the temporal-historical categories of the apocalyptic worldview. Their dualistic and world-despairing self-understanding is the only feature they share with the apocalyptic view of the world.

According to the Corinthians' worldview, the course of human destiny depends on whether one can escape from Fate or Fortune (*anankē, tychē*) and from the astrological powers that enslave people and block their entrance to the heavenly sphere. The Hellenistic age has often been called an age of anxiety[18] or an age of the failure of nerve.[19] Despite the *Pax Romana*, with its just civil order of law and the fair imperial administration of the provinces, several factors, such as the cosmopolitan atmosphere, the breakdown of traditional boundaries and the waning of ethnic religions, the syncretism of East and West, and the social insecurity and anomie of the lower classes, all combined to create a fertile soil for a gnostic climate of thought that emptied life of meaning.

This cosmological dualism is matched by an anthropology that in Platonic fashion splits body and soul, matter and spirit, and considers the physical body irrelevant, if not harmful, to people's communion with the divine and to their heavenly destiny. People feel alienated from their past and anxious about their future. Within this context the Corinthians have received the gospel with its message of the resurrection (1 Cor. 15:2; *episteusate*, v. 11). Because of the different ideological perspectives of the parties involved, an inevitable breakdown of communication occurs. The Corinthians view salvation as a present reality

18. Dodds, *Pagan and Christian in an Age of Anxiety.*
19. Murray, *Five Stages of Greek Religion,* 123–72.

(cf. 1 Cor. 1:18: *tois de sōzomenois hēmin;* cf. also 15:2); they know themselves to participate in Christ, who has conquered the powers that rule this world and has opened the door to the heavenly world of the Spirit. They have heard Paul's gospel of freedom from this world and its powers and know themselves to be sacramentally united with Christ. They accept Paul's teaching that "all things are yours . . . the world or life or death or the present or the future; all are yours, but you are Christ's, and Christ is God's" (1 Cor. 3:21-23; 6:11). This new "gnosis" (1 Cor. 8:1) enables them to maintain that "all things are lawful" (1 Cor. 6:12; 10:23), that is, all things are indifferent, compared to their new spiritual status. Moreover, their worship is one great joyful celebration of their spiritual gifts and a token of their spiritual transformation (chap. 14). Salvation means to them salvation from the body and from entanglement in a meaningless world. Therefore, the resurrection of Christ is the apex of their religiosity: Christ has conquered death and has given them eternal life through his Spirit. Resurrection power is existentially appropriated, and participation with Christ is realized through the sacraments of baptism and the Eucharist. The resurrection confirms for them the break between the ages, as Paul had said, and consequently the break with the material world, which after all is under the dominion of death and the hostile powers that Christ has overcome. When Paul spoke of "the god of this world" (2 Cor. 4:4), he apparently confirmed a radical dualism between the world of the flesh and the world of the Spirit. And if "flesh and blood cannot inherit the kingdom of God, nor the perishable inherit the imperishable" (1 Cor. 15:50), then resurrection power sheds all that is material and knows the death and resurrection of Christ as the crucial moment of leaving the "earthly tent" (2 Cor. 5:1) for the "building from God, a house not made with hands, eternal in the heavens" (2 Cor. 5:1).

The resurrection of Christ means his spiritual ascent, and those in Christ are the spiritual elite. Thus the Corinthians think of themselves as the chosen "saints" (1 Cor.

1:2, 9, 26-29), who have already been united with the heavenly Lord and now wait for physical death as the moment
of spiritual completion and of the shedding of the body,
because those who belong to Christ are already "one Spirit
with him" (1 Cor. 6:17). Within this context of spiritual
freedom and ontological participation in Christ, the Corinthians bear witness to the gospel by demonstrating their
freedom and by an ethic that proclaims in word and deed
that they have become indifferent to the world and that
history and human affairs, that is, bodily structures, cannot compromise and contaminate their mystic bond
with Christ.

In terms of their theology, then, a resurrection of the
dead (that is, a resurrection of dead bodies) is both dis-
gusting (because the body is inimical to salvation) and
superfluous, and unnecessary (because our present spiritual union with Christ constitutes the redemption of our
true self).

Paul's Argument

Paul's apocalyptic argument collides with the Hellenistic,
enthusiastic worldview of the Corinthians. He argues in 1
Cor. 15:12-22 as follows: (1) The resurrection of Christ
from the dead (*ek nekrōn*)—that is, from Sheol and the
realm of dead bodies—necessarily implies the final resurrection of all dead bodies (*anastasis nekrōn*, v. 12). (2) If
there is no final resurrection of the dead, then Christ has
not been raised (v. 13). (3) If there is no resurrection of
Christ, then there is no gospel or faith (v. 14). Verses 15,
16, and 17 recapitulate the argument: (a) If the dead are
not raised, then God has not raised Christ (vv. 15–16); and
(b) if Christ has not been raised, then there is no gospel
and no hope (vv. 17–19). Verse 20 concludes the argument
of verses 12–19: "But in fact Christ *has* been raised from
the dead, the first fruits of those who have fallen asleep."

The resurrection of Christ is no isolated or "completed"
event. Although the death of Christ is a "once and for all"
event, the same cannot be said of the resurrection. The

resurrection of Christ is not "completed" in its full meaning and consequence until the future resurrection of the dead takes place. Therefore, Christ's resurrection cannot be separated from the future apocalyptic resurrection of the dead, because this first resurrection will reach its full significance only when all the dead have been raised (cf. Rom. 1:4). Verses 20–28 underscore this claim; verse 20 and verses 23–28 prevent the Adam typology of verses 21 and 23 from being interpreted in terms of a realized eschatology. Here Paul depicts the risen Christ as the "first fruits among those who have fallen asleep," that is, as the first in a series of resurrections.[20] The resurrection of Christ is therefore not so much an event *in the midst of* history as an event that inaugurates *the end of* history. And since the resurrection of Christ is a historical and "material" event,[21] the nature and mode of the final resurrection in the age to come require further explication. Therefore, Paul discusses the question, "How are the dead raised? With what kind of body do they come?" (v. 35). Because the end of history is not simply the annihilation of history but its transformation, the resurrection will involve a body that will be raised and not just a disembodied Spirit, just as there will be a radical change for the living and not a negation of the body (cf. "but we shall all be changed," v. 51: *allagēsometha*).

The problem of the relation between this age and the age of glory causes difficulties for Paul as for any apocalyptic writer, because the discontinuity between "the spiritual body" and the earthly body of "flesh and blood" (v. 50) readily suggests a radical dualism between historical and posthistorical existence. However, Paul's insistence on "change" (v. 51), on the continuity of one's personal identity (1 Thess. 4:15), and on the somatic character of the resurrection indicates a temperate dualism and a preservation of the historical self in the midst of the end–time transformation. Paul shares, however, a lack of clarity on

20. Cf. Rom. 8:29: "the firstborn among many brethren"; Col. 1:18: "the firstborn from the dead."
21. Note the mention of witnesses in 1 Cor. 15:1–11.

this point along with apocalyptic thought in general, for which the term "glory" indicates the radically new character of eternal life in the new age.[22] But Paul's occasionally severe dualistic language about life in the age to come should not deceive us.[23] Paul's ethical imperatives, for instance, presuppose the transformation rather than the destruction of the creation: "The body is not meant for immortality, but for the Lord, and the Lord for the body. And God raised the Lord and will also raise us up by his power" (1 Cor. 6:13-14). And because the risen Christ has a "body of glory" (Phil. 3:21), which is continuous with the identity of Jesus, Paul is able to witness to the transformation of the world in the age of glory, because that age will not negate the created order but rather bring it to its eschatological destiny.

Critical Evaluation

1. The circular nature of Paul's argument in 1 Cor. 15:12-19 is obvious because for him there is a logical interaction between the two foci of the resurrection of Christ and the final apocalyptic resurrection. The cogency of the argument is based on a premise that is seemingly not open to discussion. But this premise is for the Corinthians probably the questionable postulate that determines everything else. In other words, Paul's circular argument is not convincing, because it lacks a sufficient warrant. What needs to be argued is actually taken for granted. Paul thus treats his questionable postulate as an axiomatic premise, because he considers the very question of the Corinthians an already settled matter. At issue is the necessary connection between the resurrection of Christ (which they affirm) and the futurity and somatic nature of a general resurrection of the dead (which they deny). Thus the basis for Paul's argument is "the apocalyptic connection" (1 Cor. 15:20-28). The spiritualist interpretation of the resurrection by the Corinthians, which in time became the battleground between the

22. Cf. the Apocalypse of Baruch 49–51; Mark 12:25: "they are like angels of heaven."
23. E.g., cf. 1 Cor. 6:13: "Food is meant for the stomach and the stomach for food—and God will destroy both one and the other."

church and Gnosticism and was so attractive to a Greek-Platonic thought world, is simply dismissed by Paul's apocalyptic worldview.

The Corinthians argue that because the resurrection of Christ was a resurrection from death itself, it constituted his victory over death. "Why, then," they ask, "should the resurrection of Christ from death involve a resurrection (or a resuscitation) of dead bodies?" In fact, many New Testament hymns celebrate Christ's resurrection as his victory over death and his status as world ruler (*kosmokrator*), that is, referring primarily to his exaltation and not necessarily to a "bodily" resurrection. Because these hymns link Christ's resurrection to his enthronement as Lord, they do not refer to Christ as the "first fruits" of the general resurrection from the dead.

2. Furthermore, 1 Cor. 15:45 speaks about the risen Christ as "a life-giving Spirit" (*pneuma zōopoioun*), without mentioning his "spiritual body,"[24] and Paul refers specifically to the "spiritual body" only in 1 Cor. 15:44 (cf. vv. 35-49; Phil. 3:21: *to sōma tēs doxēs autou*). The term "image" (*eikōn*, 1 Cor. 15:49) does not necessarily suggest the idea of materiality, as its adoption by later gnostics indicates. Moreover, Paul's reference to the church as "Christ" (1 Cor. 12:12) or as "the body of Christ" (1 Corinthians 12; Romans 12) might have suggested to the Corinthians that the body of the risen Lord was the church, that is, the body of believers rather than a heavenly spiritual body.

3. It is curious indeed that Paul does not formulate his argument of the "resurrection body" (1 Cor. 15:35-49) more clearly. The Corinthians could have accepted (in spiritual terms) his assertions in verses 35-41. They could easily spiritualize the analogies of seed and grain and of the different kinds of bodies. The stumbling block, however, lies in verses 42-49 where analogy shifts into an ontological claim: "It is sown a physical body, it is raised a spiritual body" (v. 44).

---

24. *Contra* the translation of the German Bible Society (1982): "der geistliche Leib" (*to pneumatikon* [v. 46]).

Thus Paul's rare mention of a "spiritual body" can lead to the possible misconception that redemption means a separation *from* the body[25] and that there is no need for a heavenly body (2 Cor. 5:6-9; Phil. 1:21-23). It is possible then that the Corinthians had not only a more consistent logic than Paul but also a foothold in Christian tradition itself for their interpretation of Christ's resurrection as his (bodiless?) exaltation to heaven. The difficulty of belief in a physical resurrection of the body is graphically attested among the Valentinian Gnostics of the second century, who called belief in a bodily resurrection "the faith of fools" (that is, the faith of "psychics"). If sacramental logic dictates that co-crucifixion with Christ means death to the body of sin and of death (Rom. 6:6; 7:24), then co-resurrection with Christ necessarily means a participation in the life of the spiritual Christ.[26] Why then does "being in Christ" have to be contradicted by a renewal of corporeality, which actually is a basic obstacle to union with God? Are not both co-crucifixion and co-resurrection profound "images" that should not be taken literally? Did not Paul himself claim in Romans 6 that our crucifixion with Christ means our death with him and our resurrection with Christ our newness of life and our future "life" with him (Rom. 6:8: *syzēsomen*)? And if the resurrection of Christ is identical with his exaltation to God's right hand that involves a shedding of his material body on the cross, what is so religiously important about a resurrection of dead bodies? Such an expectation destroys the enjoyment and meaning of the full blessing of redemption.

Thus we can assert that it is a mistake to underestimate the sophistication and viability of the "exaltation" theology of the Corinthians!

4. In 1 Corinthians 15 we have a striking example that the coherence of the gospel for Paul is not simply an experiential reality of the heart or a "Word beyond all words" that permits a translation into a multitude of worldviews.

25. But cf. Rom. 8:23.
26. Cf. chapter 5 below.

Harry Emerson Fosdick's dictum about the gospel as an "abiding experience amidst changing world views" or Rudolf Bultmann's demythologizing program for the sake of the kerygmatic address of the gospel are not true to Paul's understanding of the gospel. However applicable the gospel of "the apostle to the Gentiles" (Rom. 11:13) must be to the Gentiles in their contingent situations, it does not tolerate a worldview that cannot express those elements which are inherent in the apocalyptic worldview and which to Paul seem inherent in the truth of the gospel. Far from considering the apocalyptic worldview a husk or discardable frame, Paul insists that it belongs to the inalienable coherent core of the gospel. He closely associates the gospel with his apocalyptic perspective, for he cannot conceive of the resurrection of Christ—which the Corinthians affirm (1 Cor. 15:1, 2, 11)—apart from the general resurrection of the dead. Both stand or fall together. This is not just a problem of communication or of semantics, as if Paul could accommodate his vocabulary to a more readily acceptable position. On the contrary, for Paul the apocalyptic worldview is so interwoven with the truth of the gospel that their separation would tear the gospel apart.

This points to an important hermeneutical insight: Whenever apocalyptic categories are demoted or degraded as if they are purely culturally determined or an obsolete survival, Paul's resurrection theology is transmuted into something else, such as the immortality of the soul or our heavenly ascent, or an existential possibility or the renunciation of the created order. The rejection of apocalyptic categories therefore, has important consequences for the truth of the gospel! This holds true even if we consider them irreconcilable with our modern, scientific worldview. Paul's use of "apocalyptic categories," then, is closely interwoven with important christological, anthropological, and ethical issues.

In Paul's view the Corinthians' basic problem is their inability to relate spirituality to materiality and historical existence. According to Paul, this problem can be resolved only when the Corinthians understand and appropriate the truth of the gospel, that is, its coherent apocalyptic structure.

5. First Corinthians 15 raises the question of why Paul insists on making an apocalyptic worldview essential to the truth of the gospel. If the fundamental question in 1 Corinthians relates to the character of Christian life, that is, a life in the body by the power of the Spirit (see below), would not a theology of the cross as outlined in 1 Corinthians 1 and 2 have provided a viable solution to the Corinthian problem of a prematurely realized eschatology in the Spirit? In fact, the Gospel of John shows us the possibility of such a solution. Here the cross itself becomes the moment of the glorification of Jesus, while the Christian life is portrayed as "cross-bearing," whose reward is heavenly immortality (John 15:18-25; 16:2, 4, 33). Why then does Paul's "eschatological reservation" need an apocalyptic worldview? As the Gospel of John shows, the problem of the "already but not yet" can be resolved by a Christian life "under the cross." But this possible solution remains inadequate. A theology of the cross that is not related to the resurrection as "first fruits" of the kingdom of God and the future resurrection of the dead is in danger of neglecting the created order and the hope in God's final cosmic triumph over his rebellious creation. In that case it becomes all too easy to transform the theology of the cross into a form of passion mysticism and to collapse the resurrection into a purely intellectual "event," that is, to understand the resurrection solely as the *meaning* of the cross.[27] The Gospel of John actually demonstrates the limitation of such a theology of the cross, because—notwithstanding its emphasis on Christian life under the cross—the cross becomes the secret hour of glory, the "gateway" to heaven, and it ceases to have cosmic-eschatological meaning for a fallen world.

Therefore, in Paul the cross is firmly embedded in the apocalyptic framework of the resurrection of Christ, so

27. Bultmann, *The New Testament and Mythology*, 36.

that the proleptic victory in the cross and resurrection of Christ signals the future public victory of God in the final resurrection of the dead. Christian life in the body by the Spirit is indeed life under the cross. Thus "we proclaim the Lord's death" in the Eucharist (1 Cor. 11:26). But life under the cross is not celebrated as if suffering has become acceptable or "good" in the gospel. To the contrary, suffering awaits the triumph of God, and so Paul adds in the same verse, "we proclaim the Lord's death *until he comes*" (1 Cor. 11:26). The "eschatological reservation" in Paul looks forward to the future resurrection of the dead, so that the present paradox of "victory *in the midst of death*" (2 Cor. 4:11) is nourished by a hope for the transformation of the entire creation, that is, in the victory *over* death. Only then the song of triumph will be heard: "Death is swallowed up in victory. O death, where is thy victory? O death where is thy sting?" (1 Cor. 15:54, 55).

"The redemption of the body" (Rom. 8:23) is not a redemption "from the body" but a redemption of the total "body" of creation (Rom. 8:21). And so Paul concludes 1 Corinthians 15 with this exhortation: "Therefore, my beloved brethren, be steadfast, immovable, always abounding in the work of the Lord, knowing that in the Lord your labor is not in vain" (15:58).

By way of summary, the apocalyptic worldview is the fundamental carrier of Paul's thought. Without it his basic christological focus becomes distorted. Without it the design of Paul's theology shifts from Christ as the "first fruits" to Christ as the total "fullness of God" (Col. 1:19), that is, to Christ as the completed and final revelation of God, which exhausts all of God's glory and triumph.

The "material content" (*Sachgehalt*) of the gospel in Paul cannot be separated from the necessary "linguistic medium" (*Sprachgestalt*) of apocalyptic thought. In this sense it would be a mistake to demythologize apocalyptic thought patterns or to regard them as incidental linguistic "husks" that can be transposed into a nonapocalyptic metaphysic. The post-Pauline history of the church clearly shows how the gospel itself was jeopardized when nonapocalyptic thought forms became its hermeneutical carrier.

THE CROSS OF CHRIST AND
THE DEMONIC POWERS

Paul's interpretation of Christ's death is imbedded within an apocalyptic framework in the following ways: (1) The death of Christ strips the apocalyptic forces of their power. Therefore, it is to be understood not only as an act of moral atonement but also as an apocalyptic event. (2) Christ's death represents God's final judgment on the old age. Moreover, Paul not only intensifies this Jewish apocalyptic motif but also transforms it: The death of Christ changes both the condition of life after death and the elitist views of Jewish apocalyptic. (3) Furthermore, the death of Christ is closely related to his resurrection. Since the resurrection of Christ is an apocalyptic and cosmic event that inaugurates the cosmic triumph of God, it draws the death of Christ into its apocalyptic orbit. (4) Finally, Paul interprets the saving (soteriological) effects of the death and resurrection of Christ not only in a sequential-consecutive way (as in apocalyptic) but also in a dialectical manner. These points will be elaborated in what follows.

The Apocalyptic Framework of Paul's
Interpretation of the Death of Christ

1. For Paul the predominant apocalyptic powers are those ontological forces that determine the human condition and that encompass the "field" of death, sin, the law, and the flesh. This field comprises an alliance of powers under the sovereign rule of death. All these powers have their own particular sphere or dominion: Human beings are "under the power of sin" (*hamartia,* Rom. 3:9) or "under the power of the law" (*nomos,* Rom. 6:15); sin (*hamartia*) "reigns" (Rom. 5:21) and death (*thanatos*) "reigns" (Rom. 6:9; cf. 5:17); the flesh (*sarx*) has a "mindset" of its own (Rom. 8:5-7) or "desires" (Gal. 5:17). This field operates as an interrelated whole; its forces cannot be genetically delineated, and no single power can be viewed in isolation from

the others. In Romans 7, for example, sin enters the human scene from the outside with help from the law, and the alliance between sin and the law brings about people's death (v. 11). But from another perspective, people are already sold under sin before the law enters the picture, because they are carnal by nature (*sarkinos,* 7:14; cf. 5:12). In this case the law only confirms what people already are (5:20). Again, in Rom. 8:3 the law is not the beachhead for sin as in 7:8, 11, but is infected by the flesh (*sarx*) and thus incapable of resisting the power of sin. How, we may ask, can a person be both determined by sin and thus unable to fulfill the law, and at the same time be innocent of sin until the law provides sin an opportunity to enter from the outside?

Death, on the one hand, is "the wages of sin" (Rom. 6:23), so that sin is the agent and death its consequence. But, on the other hand, death can also be characterized as the agent and sin its instrument (1 Cor. 15:56). In any case, death is actually the primal power; it is "the last enemy" (1 Cor. 15:26) in the network of interconnected apocalyptic forces. The antithesis between the two ages can be summed up as the opposition between "the reign of death" and "the reign of life" (Rom. 5:17, 21). And death remains in some way the signature of this world, even after its allies—the law, the flesh, and sin—have been defeated in the death and resurrection of Christ (1 Cor. 15:24-26; cf. chapter 5 below). The *death of Christ* shatters the alliance of the apocalyptic powers and signals the imminent overthrow of death, "the last enemy" (cf. Rom. 6:7-10; 7:4-6; 8:35-39; 1 Cor. 2:6-8; 15:26). This is why it is an apocalyptic event and not merely an act of sacrificial love that evokes in us a moral sentiment and a good disposition. Colossians interprets Paul's understanding of Christ's death correctly on this point: "He disarmed the principalities and powers and made a public example of them, triumphing over them in him" (Col. 2:15; cf. Eph. 1:20-22). Christ's death truly constitutes the eschatological judgment of the apocalyptic powers. "The rulers of this age" have "crucified the Lord of glory" (1 Cor. 2:8); the rebellion of the world and its powers against God reaches its climax in the death of Christ. But it is precisely in the cross of Christ that the world itself is judged: "for since, in the wisdom of God, the world did not know God through wisdom, it pleased God through the folly of what we preach to save those who believe" (1 Cor. 1:21). In that sense, God's wrath culminates in the death of Christ: "These [the Jews] have killed both the Lord Jesus and the prophets. . . . God's wrath has come upon them until the end" (1 Thess. 2:15-16, trans. mine). And God's apocalyptic judgment in the death of Christ will be confirmed in the last judgment, because those who do not believe the word of the cross will "perish" (*apollyesthai*, 1 Cor. 1:18; 2 Cor. 2:15). "Their end is perdition" (*apōleia*, Phil. 3:19; cf. 1:28) and "sudden destruction" (*aiphnidios olethros*, 1 Thess. 5:3).

Paul reinterprets the traditional Christian conception of the righteousness of God—as a covenant renewal, as an expiation by Christ, as Christ the Paschal Lamb (Rom. 3:24-26; 1 Cor. 5:7), or as the sacrificial blood of Christ (Rom. 3:24-25; 5:9)—in terms of his understanding of the death of Christ as the judgment on the powers of this age. The language of the tradition does not sufficiently express for Paul the "cosmic" significance of the death of Christ, that is, his victory over death and its allies of sin, the law, and the flesh (cf. Gal. 3:13; 4:4-5; Rom. 6:1-10; 8:3; 2 Cor. 5:20). The death and resurrection of Christ marks the discontinuity between the old and new age because it breaks history apart into the era of the Old Adam and that of the eschatological Adam (Rom. 5:12-21).

Moreover, the death of Christ does not refer primarily to the death of an innocent suffering martyr, which evokes remorse and moral cleansing; it does not mean a new moral beginning for the "old" person or primarily the forgiveness of sins so that one can begin again with a clean slate. To the contrary, the death of Christ addresses itself to sin as a cosmic power, that is, to the human condition "under the power of sin" (Rom. 3:9). Sin's rule over the world is destroyed by the death of Christ, and thus it has not only a moral but also an ontological meaning: "If anyone is in Christ, then he is a new creation: the old has passed away . . . the new has come" (2 Cor. 5:7; Gal. 6:15).

2. Paul's emphasis on the wrath and judgment of God both affirms and transforms Jewish apocalyptic thinking. It affirms it because Paul, like the apocalyptic writers of his time, views God's wrath and judgment less as his purifying chastisement or as his divine pedagogy than as a cosmic-apocalyptic event. This is clearly attested in Rom. 1:18-32, where God is portrayed as the apocalyptic harvester whose wrath pronounces his final judgment on history.

However, at the same time, Paul transforms Jewish apocalyptic because he structures, for example, the relation of particularism to universalism in the age to come in a different mood and mode. He dismisses the notion of an apocalyptic exclusivism, with its reward of the faithful and its celebration of the eternal condemnation of the godless. Thus for Paul, in contrast to John's Apocalypse, there is no room for a vengeance motif or for a rejoicing in the torture of God's enemies. He not only rejects this motif of Jewish martyrdom theology but also, because of the Christ-event, radically changes the definition of faith and its reward. The Jewish apocalyptic resurrection of the dead involves a change from mortal to glorious bodies, which is the reward for the faith and obedience of "the righteous."[28] Paul can also speak about resurrection life as a reward for obedience (1 Cor. 3:12-15), but this idea dwindles before his prevailing insight that only the death and resurrection of Christ can save Jews and Gentiles alike from the death sentence of the wrath and judgment of God (Rom. 1:18-3:20). In other words, the death of Christ is the proleptic division between this age of judgment and death and the new age of life; it is an abyss that no one can escape and before which all humankind comes to naught.

28. Cf. the Apocalypse of Baruch, 49–51.

In Judaism sin and death are powers that have lost their cutting edge for those who are faithful to the Torah. Paul reformulates this conception by radicalizing not only God's wrath but also the powers of sin and death ("the last enemy"). The death of Christ becomes for Paul the focus of God's judgment, and faith in Christ's death for us will be the decisive criterion at the future last judgment. Because all have sinned, all must die. Therefore, the death of Christ signifies the apocalyptic judgment on all humankind, and his resurrection signifies the *sola gratia* of new life for all (cf. Rom. 3:23; 5:18).

3. Paul's apocalyptic-cosmic interpretation of the death of Christ is rooted in its inseparable connection with the resurrection of Christ. When that connection is misinterpreted, both the cross and resurrection lose their "cosmic"-apocalyptic meaning and collapse into either a theology of glory or an individualistic theology of the cross. In both cases, the "apocalyptic connection" between the Christ-event and the future triumph of God is severed and displaced by a Christonomism that entails a false perspective on both the death and resurrection of Christ.

4. The death and resurrection of Christ are first of all *consecutive* events in Paul.

> We know that Christ being raised from the dead will never die again; death no longer has dominion over him [twice *ouketi*]. The death he died he died to sin, once for all [*ephapax*], but the life he lives he lives to God. (Rom. 6:9-10)

> For he was crucified [past tense] in weakness, but lives [present tense] by the power of God. (2 Cor. 13:4)[29]

> But if we have died with Christ, we believe that we shall also live with him. (Rom. 6:8)

> Since, therefore, we are now justified by his blood, much more shall we be saved by him from the wrath of God. (Rom. 5:9)

This consecutive, linear interpretation betrays the influence of apocalyptic thought: After the judgment of death comes

---

29. Lietzmann, *An die Korinther* II, 160.

the glory of the resurrection and the new life, just as the grain follows the death of the seed (1 Cor. 15:36-38). Thus whereas the cross accentuates the judgment and death of the old age, the resurrection of Christ announces the dawn of the new age to come. In this context we can understand why the "rabbinic" language of sacrifice and atonement is unsatisfactory for Paul. Although the ideas of judgment and forgiveness are common in rabbinic literature, it is incapable of stating the new ontological status of the new life that succeeds God's judgment in the death of Christ. To be sure, according to rabbinic understanding forgiveness means acquittal of punishment, but not the destruction of the power of sin or the "new creation" that comes through participation in the resurrection life of Christ.

The linear interpretation of death and resurrection stresses the finality of the death of Christ, that is, the "once and for all" character of the destruction of the forces of evil. However, the resurrection emphasizes a different kind of finality, because it is incomplete apart from its consummation in the new age. In other words, there is a soteriological identity of Christians with Christ in their co-crucifixion with him, but this soteriological identity does not apply to the resurrection of Christ. Indeed, Christ *has died* and *has been raised*. Believers *have also died* with Christ, but whereas Christ has been raised, Christians *have not yet been raised* (Rom. 6:5-8). The resurrection of Christ constitutes the first event in a series to come, which will be completed only at the general resurrection of the dead. Christ, therefore, is the "first fruits" (*aparchē*) of the general resurrection (1 Cor. 15:20). Thus the symmetry between the death of Christ and his resurrection breaks down in its application to Christian life (see below, chapter 5). There is indeed both a conjunction and a disjunction here: Christ and the Christians are *conjoined* in their death to sin; but they are *disjoined* in their victory over death itself, since Christ's present victory over death is still a matter of hope for Christians.

It is striking that in Paul *a dialectical* relation between the death and resurrection of Christ intersects the *linear-consecutive* relation. And this may well be Paul's unique contribution to the theology of the cross. Life is not just life *after* death, but life *in the midst of* death, just as "power" not only succeeds "weakness" (1 Cor. 15:43) but also manifests itself as "weakness": "For when I am weak, then I am strong" (2 Cor. 12:10). The catalogs of "dangerous situations" (*peristaseis* = crisis situations; cf. 1 Cor. 4:9-13; 2 Cor. 4:7-12; 6:3-10; Rom. 8:35-39) claim that life and power are not only present *after* or *in spite of* human weakness, but that they manifest themselves *as* weakness itself. Christian life is truly cruciform: "For while we live we are always being given up to death for Jesus' sake, so that the life of Jesus may be manifested in our mortal flesh. So death is at work in us, but life in you" (2 Cor. 4:11-12).

The main body of Romans (chaps. 5–8) provides an important commentary on the linear and dialectical interaction of death and life as grounded in the death and resurrection of Christ. The love of God in the death of Christ causes us to "rejoice in our hope of sharing the glory of God" (Rom. 5:2), a theme that is subsequently elaborated in Rom. 8:18-39. But this hope in the coming glory is intersected by a "rejoicing in our sufferings" (Rom. 5:3; 8:17, 37), not only because "life" succeeds suffering, but also because "life" itself is experienced as suffering: "and if [we are] children, then heirs, heirs of God and fellow heirs with Christ, provided we suffer with him in order that we may also be glorified with him" (Rom. 8:17). Moreover, Paul often refrains from assigning death and resurrection to distinct spheres, as if the death of Christ stands only for God's judgment and his resurrection only for eternal life. In texts where the resurrection is not explicitly mentioned (Rom. 5:6-8; 8:32; Gal. 2:20; 2 Cor. 5:15), the love of God and its life-giving power frequently occur (see below, chapter 5). Likewise, the salvation event in Christ sometimes appears in formulas that express the "sending" of Christ, where there is no clear reference to the death and resurrection of Christ (Gal. 4:4) or where such a reference must be inferred from the text (Rom. 8:3; 2 Cor. 5:21).

The Theology of the Cross

Although Paul considers the death and resurrection of Christ as two separate events, he often interprets them as if they have a single meaning. The context determines in each case whether the elements of judgment or those of love and life prevail in a given passage. This is especially true of Paul's theology of the cross, which is his unique contribution to the interpretation of the death and resurrection of Christ.

Contrary to widespread opinion, a theology of the cross is rare in the New Testament. It must be distinguished not only from a theology of the death and resurrection of Christ, but also from a theology of Christ's suffering. The interactions among these various forms of reflection on the death of Christ do not permit us to blend them, for each has its own distinct significance. The motif of "the cross" never appears within the traditional sequence of "he died and rose again/was raised." The only passage where Paul probably interprets Christ's sacrificial death in terms of the "cross" is 1 Cor. 1:13: "Was Paul crucified for you?" Contrary to our common speech about the "cross and resurrection," there is no "cross–resurrection" formula in Paul. The focus on the death of Christ in the terminology of the "cross" is often so exclusive that in most contexts no explicit "life" terminology relieves its darkness and judgment. This observation is confirmed by the fact that "the cross" is never associated with the sacrificial formulas "hyper" and "peri" (= "in behalf of"). While "death" (*thanatos*) and "dying" (*apothnēskein*) are regularly connected with the resurrection and frequently with the motif of Christ's sacrificial death, the latter motif is absent in the terminology of the cross.[30] Because the terminology of the

---

30. But cf. Gal. 6:14: "But far be it from me to glory except in the cross of our Lord Jesus Christ, *by which* [*di' hou*] the world has been crucified to me, and I to the world."

"cross" and "to crucify" infrequently occurs in Paul, the specificity of its occurrence suggests its profound meaning, just as the specifically Pauline interpretation of "grace" (*charis*) is quantitatively inversely related to its qualitative importance.

Theologies of Suffering and the Theology of the Cross

The terminology of the cross is never directly associated with human suffering or with the suffering of Christ and God. A word of caution is necessary at this point. The cross of Christ does not permit us to interpret it in terms of a passion mysticism, a meditation on the wounds of Christ, or in terms of a spiritual absorption into the sufferings of Christ.[31] Paul never sanctifies or hallows death, pain, and suffering. He takes no masochistic delight in suffering. The death of Christ is efficacious only because it stands within the radius of the victory of the resurrection (Rom. 6:8, 10; 14:9; 2 Cor. 13:4; 1 Thess. 4:14).

Although the death of Christ qualifies the resurrection of Christ as that of the crucified one, the death of Christ does not in and by itself inaugurate the new age or by itself sanctify and legitimize suffering and death as the way in which God exercises his lordship in an evil world, that is, as suffering love. There is no Christomonism of the cross, no passion mysticism, and no patri-passionism in Paul. The issue of the suffering love of God, as opposed to his *apatheia* (incapability of suffering), must not be read into Paul's thought. The spheres of suffering and death are confined by Paul to this world and hence are not constituent aspects of God's being. The glory of God, which will encompass creation in the future, is not contaminated by— or coordinated with—notions of the virtues of suffering, pain, or death. Paul does not create a monogram of the cross in heaven, as displayed, for instance, in the S. Giovanni Bapistry in Naples.[32] The glory of God is instead

31. Cf. the *conformitas crucis* in medieval theology.
32. Cf. Ethelbert Stauffer, *Die Theologie des Neuen Testaments*, 356, figure 111.

characterized by "imperishability" (*aphtharsia*) and "immortality" (*athanasia*, 1 Cor. 15:53; cf. also 15:42). The "spiritual body" (*sōma pneumatikon*, 1 Cor. 15:44) implies the future elimination of the mortal and suffering character of Christian life in this world (Rom. 8:11). And even Jesus' present lordship in glory is not that of a Jesus who "will be in agony until the end of the world" (Pascal),[33] but rather it has a status in which "death [and suffering] has no longer dominion over him" (Rom. 6:9). The image of a risen Christ who in heaven bears the marks of the crucified one may perhaps be a necessary consequence of a hermeneutical reflection on Paul's thought, but it cannot be ascribed to the historical Paul himself.

Paul is in many ways unique among other early so-called "theologians of the cross" such as Ignatius, 1 Peter, Mark, and John. Whereas the vocabulary of suffering and a notion of the "Imitation of Christ"—or at least the idea of Jesus' passion as paradigm of Christian discipleship—are prominent themes in these early writers, in Paul the motif of Christian suffering is limited to only a few passages (Phil. 1:29; 1 Thess. 2:14; 2 Cor. 1:6; Rom. 8:17) and never refers to the death of Christ. Thus he never says, "Christ suffered and was raised." And although the cross is a main theme in the Gospel of John, John fuses cross and resurrection in such a way that the cross is no longer a scandal but the gateway to glory (John 12:27-33). Paul, however, presents the cross both as a scandal and as the hour of Christ's weakness (1 Cor. 1:23, 25; 2 Cor. 13:4).

For Paul the cross constitutes the climax of his apocalyptic interpretation of the death and resurrection of Christ. It occurs exclusively in three contexts: (a) the cross and wisdom (1 Cor. 1:17-18, 23; 2:2, 8); (b) the cross and the law (Gal. 2:20; 3:1; 5:11; 6:14); and (c) the cross and "the new creation" (Gal. 5:24; 6:14; Rom. 6:6).

In the contexts of wisdom and the law, the apocalyptic element of negation dominates. Wisdom and the law are

---

33. Cf. Pascal, "Le Mystère de Jésus" in *Pensées:* "Jésus sera en agonie jusqu'á a fin du monde. Il ne faut pas dormir pendant ce temps-là."

both structures of this age, normative powers for both
Greeks and Jews. They are symbolic abbreviations for the
highest values of "the civilized and religious world." In
the light of the cross, however, wisdom and the law sym-
bolize for Paul "the world," because both fall equally and
impartially under its judgment. The utter bleakness of the
cross predominates here; the motif of vicarious suffering
(*hyper, peri*) is completely absent, just as there is no reference to the suffering love of God or to Christian participation in suffering as a mark of discipleship. Just as the
passion story of the Gospel of Mark heightens the themes
of betrayal, abandonment, and judgment (Mark 15), so
Paul stresses the cross as the apex of God's wrath and
judgment. It is not the world's "finest hour" but its "last
hour." Thus the cross negates and judges the worlds of
religion and culture: it contradicts wisdom (1 Cor. 1:18);
it crucifies the law and the world (Gal. 2:20; 6:14); it arouses
public hostility (Phil. 3:18); it is foolishness (1 Cor. 1:18);
a scandal to Jews and folly to Gentiles (1 Cor. 1:23; Gal.
5:11); and it is truly a manifestation of weakness (1 Cor.
1:25; 2 Cor. 13:4).

Nevertheless, the cross contains not only the aspect of
"death," but also that of "resurrection" and "life." Although this last aspect is only implicitly present, passages
such as Phil. 2:8-11, 2 Cor. 13:4, Rom. 6:6, and Gal. 3:1-
5 show that the cross signifies both judgment and life. It
is the abyss for the world, but on the other side of the
abyss of death and judgment there is "life." Thus the cross
is the apocalyptic turning point of history. Though it over-
whelmingly focuses upon the negative side of God's future
triumph, the cross proclaims not only "negation," but also
a joyful "affirmation." In Gal. 6:15, for example, the "new
creation" immediately follows upon the crucifixion of the
old world (Gal. 6:14). As in the Gospel of John (12:31),
the cross is the judgment of the world. It can be acknowledged as God's judgment and saving power only by a
radical "perceptual shift" on the part of those who are
"called" and "chosen" (1 Cor. 1:26-29), for the cross is and
remains foolishness and a scandal (Gal. 5:11) as long as

Christians live in this world. Thus the cross is not a "pseu-do-obstacle" or a "pseudo-foolishness" that only a deep gnosis can comprehend as a secret wisdom. The cross of Christ is indeed "once for all," but the scandal of the cross is not once for all eliminated; it must always be reappropriated in the cruciform life of Christians.

The theology of the cross embodies Paul's unique apocalyptic interpretation of the Christ-event. The future age already dawns in the cross just as the old age comes to naught in it. And so the cross directs Christians to their present mission in the world; they are not to flee from the world to a premature resurrection glory in the Spirit. Therefore, the cross is a reminder of the "now" of life in Christ and of its hidden victory. It has this power because it points to the future triumph of God, when the glorious resurrection of all creation will not only confirm but also succeed the cruciform existence of Christians. Then the *dialectic* of cross and resurrection in this life will be transformed into the *sequence* of resurrection life *after* our cruciform life in the final victory of God.

CHRISTIAN LIFE AND THE CHURCH:
THE APPROPRIATION AND PRACTICE OF
THE GOSPEL IN THE HORIZON OF HOPE

Fundamental Considerations

The "indicative" of God's redemptive act in Christ is inextricably linked to the ethical imperative ("therefore," Rom. 6:12). And yet the interaction between these two elements of Paul's thought does not constitute a timeless dogmatic system, but is directly related to the "timely" contingency of Paul's argumentation.

Judaizers and Jewish Christians, for example, must hear the "indicative" of the eschatological "now" of God's redemption in Christ, because they behave as if the Messiah has not already come. They do not recognize that God's act in Christ renders superfluous "the works of the law" and every human striving for acceptance in the last judgment. Thus it comes as no surprise that the apocalyptic

future plays a subordinate role in Romans 1–4 and practically no role at all in Galatians 1–6.

On the other hand, Hellenistic Christians must be alerted
to the "imperative" of Christian life, because their exclusive
celebration of the "indicative"—that is, of participation in
Christ—threatens to dissolve the necessary correlation of
the indicative and the imperative. In this context Paul emphasizes the "not yet" of Christian life, that is, the so-called
eschatological reservation, in conjunction with a specific
ethic, which is grounded not only in the indicative of the
Christ-event but also in the future indicative of the last
judgment and the final victory of God.[34] However, the
contingency of the gospel does not mean "different strokes
for different folks," that is, a different gospel for different
occasions. Though particular circumstances require a particular hermeneutical contingency, they are not allowed to
alter the coherence of the gospel. Therefore we must reject
a "two-crater theory" (Schweitzer)[35] and an "audience theory" (Lütgert),[36] because a particular "crater" does not
represent the coherence of the gospel and a particular "audience" does not create a different coherent center of the
gospel.

In this context it should be emphasized that the coherence
of the gospel is not identical with any one of the various
metaphors Paul uses to make the truth of the gospel effective and intelligible in a particular sociocultural context.
The continuing debate about the center of Paul's thought
as either "justification by faith" or "eschatological mysticism in Christ," or as a hierarchical structure of some
kind, where one metaphor dominates the others, deals with
wrong alternatives, because the real center of Paul's gospel
lies in the lordship of Christ as it anticipates the final triumph of God. Paul interprets the apocalyptic coherence of
the gospel in a variety of metaphors that interact and in-
terweave to form an organic whole. Consequently, a developmental theory or an atomistic analysis of the various
metaphors bypasses Paul's hermeneutical intent.

34. Cf., e.g., Rom. 13:12; Gal. 6:8; 1 Cor. 4:5.
35. Schweitzer, *The Mysticism of Paul the Apostle.*
36. Lütgert, *Gesetz und Geist.*

Gerd Theissen has made an important contribution to Paul's soteriology with his structural analysis of Paul's "transfer symbolism."[37] According to Theissen, two basic symbolic structures determine Paul's soteriology: a socio-morphic interaction symbolism and a physiomorphic transformation symbolism. Whereas the first symbolism refers to a soteriology of redemptive action, reflected in the prepositions *hypo* ("under") and *hyper* ("on behalf of"), the second symbolism focuses rather on a soteriology of redemptive participation, characterized by the prepositions *hos* ("just as"), *syn* ("with") and *en* (*Christo*) ("in Christ"). Theissen's analysis shows how the different metaphors are interwoven and penetrate one another. It also makes clear that the various levels of interaction among the symbols do not permit a separation between a so-called juristic and a mystical language.

The Spirit and the Glory of God

Paul's interpretation of the Spirit clarifies for his Hellenistic churches a frequent misconception. Although the Spirit is indeed the power (*dynamis*) of the messianic age in the present, its power is qualified by its close connection with the death and resurrection of Christ, so that it (1) is preliminary to the final glory of God; (2) is operative amid the embattled ethical situation of believers in the world; and (3) is cruciform, because the Spirit is defined by the resurrection power of a crucified Messiah.

This demarcation between the Spirit and the future consummation is difficult to draw in Hellenistic culture. The dualistic anthropology of the Hellenistic world with its division of "Spirit" and "body" (*pneuma* vs. *soma; nous* vs. *soma*) favors a fusion of the divine and the human spirit. As early as Philo the ecstatic presence of the prophetic Spirit forces the mind to leave the body.[38] Moreover, the Hellenistic world thinks of "Spirit" as a heavenly substance—however ethereal—because all power is conceived

37. Theissen, "Soteriologische Symbolik in den paulinischen Schriften."
38. Philo, *Quis rerum divinarum heres,* 265.

in terms of a material substratum. The Spirit functions then to deify believers; it transports them into the heavenly world of God's kingdom and separates them from any entanglements with the inferior material body. They already consider themselves "spiritualized" and lifted out of history. Paul argues in Corinth in a setting in which the gift of the Spirit is understood as the complete presence of the kingdom of God (1 Cor. 4:8) and as the power that segregates the *pneumatikoi* ("bearers of the Spirit") from the rest of the world. Paul's task here is to interpret the Spirit against its identification with the kingdom of God, for in Corinth spiritual gifts (*ta pneumatika,* 1 Cor. 12:1-11) have become an exhibition before the world of the believers' separation from the world. In this sense the theology of the Corinthians resembles that of the Gospel of John. Because John links the resurrection of Christ with the gift of the Spirit and the parousia, he interprets the kingdom of God as the presence of the Spirit (John 13–17). Such a hermeneutic transforms the gulf between "the fallen world" and the church into an abyss, so that the church becomes, as it were, a pneumatic elite that gathers like-minded pneumatics unto itself and surrenders its redemptive mission to the world.

The significance of Paul's interpretation of the Spirit lies in his ability to distinguish clearly between the kingdom of God and the Spirit without either relaxing their dynamic relationship (as in Acts) or fusing them (as in John). When in the post-Pauline period the Spirit became detached from its intimate relationship to the kingdom of God, it lost its eschatological dynamic character as "first fruits" (*aparchē*) and "down payment" (*arrabōn*) (cf. Rom. 8:23; 2 Cor. 1:22, 5:5). Now the work of the Spirit became either a momentary inspirational force and the power of prophetic prediction or an entity that was placed under the control of the church and was guided into institutional channels.[39]

Whenever the Spirit is fused with the kingdom of God, a "Corinthian theology" ensues. The Spirit is now no longer related to its Hebrew meaning "wind in motion" or

39. Cf. the Pastoral letters.

"life-giving power" but is absorbed into Hellenistic metaphysics as a substance of the divine world "above" that manifests itself as the epiphany of the divine in miraculous events and transforms human beings into "divine men" (*theioi andres*) and/or "royal prophets."[40]

In Paul, however, the Spirit has an apocalyptic mooring because it is determined by its relation to the future glory of God (*doxa tou theou;* Hebrew: *kabod*), that is, the "weight," majesty, and honor of God.[41] *Kabod* in Judaism is a synonym of the *shekinah,* that is, the presence of God in the temple or in the rabbinic study of the Torah. However, it refers primarily to the quality of the messianic age, to the glorious life of the kingdom of God.

The movement of the argument in Romans 8 clearly shows how Paul understands the Spirit. In verses 1–16 the Spirit is a present ontological reality that marks Christian life as the antithesis of Spirit and flesh. Nevertheless, the Spirit (*pneuma*) receives its power from the future glory of God (*doxa*), that is, from the content of the hope, which will embrace the whole of creation (vv. 17–30). The connection between "the glory" (*doxa*) and "the Spirit" (*pneuma*) demonstrates the ontological character of the Spirit. "Glory" is not just a liturgical metaphor for the majesty and honor of God, as when Paul speaks about "glorifying the God and Father of our Lord Jesus Christ" (*doxazein;* Rom. 15:6), but also contains, like the Old Testament *kabod,* a physical connotation that refers to the ontological character of the new age.[42] The Spirit as our new domain foreshadows our final freedom and glory; and the Spirit as the power of the ethical life propels us toward that glory by overcoming the powers of this world: "For the desires of the flesh are against the Spirit, and the desires of the Spirit are against the flesh; for these are opposed to each other, to prevent you from doing what you would. But if

---

40. Cf. Philo, *Vita Mosis.*
41. This, in particular, is a feature of the Old Testament priestly tradition.
42. Cf. 1 Cor. 15:43: "It is sown in dishonor, it is raised in glory"; further, 1 Cor. 15:44; Phil. 3:21; Rom. 8:21.

you are led by the Spirit you are not under the law" (Gal. 5:17-18).

The Spirit and the Body

Because Paul opposes "the flesh" (*sarx*) to "the Spirit" (2 Cor. 10:3; Rom. 7:5; 8:4, 9, 12; Gal. 5:24), believers are no longer "in the flesh, but in the Spirit" (Rom. 8:9) and serve "in the new life of the Spirit" (Rom. 7:6). For this reason "the flesh" is never associated with the Spirit (but cf. 2 Cor. 4:11), whereas the body (*soma*) is necessarily related to "the Spirit" (1 Cor. 6:19; cf. 3:16).

When Paul speaks of life in the Spirit, he does not mean an otherworldly life but rather a life within the contours of our historical world. The locus of the Spirit's activity is "in the body" for "other bodies" in the context of "the body of Christ" (Rom. 12:4; 1 Cor. 12:12-27). Käsemann has argued correctly against Bultmann that the human being *is* not only a body, but also *has* a body: There is a material dimension to the body that links it to the whole created order. According to Käsemann,[43] we are not disembodied selves but embodied selves; the body expresses our solidarity with the stuff of creation, so that the apocalyptic "redemption of our body" (Rom. 8:23) will coincide with the redemption of creation (Rom. 8:21).

What does it mean to have the Spirit in the body? It is crucial for Paul in two respects, because it expresses (1) the solidarity of Christians with an unredeemed world and (2) the ethical seriousness of Christians in their engagement with the world.

1. Paul adopts an expression unique in the New Testament: "the mortal body" (*sōma thnēton*). The significance of this term lies in its distinction not only from "the body of sin" (*sōma tēs hamartias*, Rom. 6:6) and "the flesh" (*sarx*, Gal. 5:24; cf. also "the body of the flesh" [*sōma tēs sarkos*], Col. 2:11), but also from the "spiritual body" (*sōma pneumatikon*, 1 Cor. 15:44). "The mortal body" expresses our historical existence "between the times," during which we

---

43. Käsemann, *Perspectives on Paul*, 26.

no longer live "in the body of sin" and do not as yet have the "spiritual body." Thus the multivalent contextual meaning of the term "mortal body" yields a rich meaning: on the one hand, the Spirit's activity in the mortal body means that we can praise and honor God in our "bodies" (1 Cor. 6:20; Rom. 12:1); on the other hand, the body is subjected to death, decay, and weakness and can even be called "flesh" (2 Cor. 4:11). This ambivalence explains the problem of our personal identity or "continuity" amid the discontinuity posed by the several dimensions of "death" in the stages of salvation. Thus it answers the difficult problem of continuity and discontinuity of "bodies," that is, their permanence and transience.

Our transfer in baptism from the realm of the "body of sin" or "the flesh" to that of the Spirit implies a radical discontinuity between the "old man" (*palaios anthrōpos,* Rom. 6:6) and "the new creation" (*kainē ktisis,* Gal. 6:15; 2 Cor. 5:17; cf. Rom. 6:4). Likewise, the transfer to "the spiritual body" in the final resurrection of the dead marks a radical discontinuity, because according to Paul "flesh and blood cannot inherit the kingdom of God" (1 Cor. 15:50). "The (mortal) body" now functions as the principle of continuity between the discontinuity of the ages, because the body remains the carrier of our personal identity. And this occurs despite the fact that not only our crucifixion with Christ in baptism but also our death before the parousia (or our radical change; cf. 1 Cor. 15:51) involve a radical change of both our former bodies and our present bodies.

Therefore, "the mortal body" is an "interim" reality. Although we, as mortal bodies, are no longer "the body of sin" and not yet "the spiritual body," we are bodies that are subject both to the rule of the Spirit and to the rule of death. As "mortal bodies" we are linked with the whole mortal "body" of creation as we wait for our final redemption, and thus we groan in the Spirit along with the groaning of the creation for the future glory of God. As a result the "body" metaphor has a cosmic-universal connotation: "the redemption of our bodies" (Rom. 8:23) is not an individualistic matter but involves the redemption of the total body of the created order (Rom. 8:19-21).

2. Because the Spirit is the power behind the moral life and not a reward for "the works of the law," its function is unthinkable apart from life in the body. Believers are exhorted to proclaim the victory of the Spirit in the world: "glorify God in your body" (1 Cor. 6:20). And Paul insists that "the body is not meant for immortality, but for the Lord, and the Lord for the body," because "God raised the Lord and will also raise us up by his power" (1 Cor. 6:13, 14; cf. 3:16; 6:19). Because life in the Spirit is life in the body and because the "deeds of the body" (Rom. 8:13) will be judged "before the judgment seat of Christ" (2 Cor. 5:10), Paul appeals for a body that is blameless on the day of Christ (Phil. 1:10). Therefore he trains his body like an athlete (1 Cor. 9:27) and presses on "toward the goal for the prize of the call from above of God in Christ Jesus" (Phil. 3:14, my trans.).

Because the Spirit is directly connected not only with the coming glory of God but also with the life of believers "in the body," a new reflection on the ethical problem of the indicative and imperative in Paul's theology becomes necessary. For the imperative is not a "timeless" application of the "once and for all" redemptive indicative (*ephapax*) of the Christ-event. Rather, the imperative moves between the indicative of the Christ-event and its confirmation and consummation in God's coming glory. The Christian's progress is, to be sure, a "regress" to the foot of the cross of Christ (cf. Luther), but it is also a progress in the body under the guidance of the Spirit toward the end of the pilgrimage in "the promised land." Thus the justification of the sinner and the sanctification of the Christian cohere in Paul's thought because the christological indicative does not swallow up God's future apocalyptic indicative at the end of time. The last judgment does not pale before the forensic judgment of our justification in Christ, and the indicative of the Christ-event does not constitute "the mid-point of time," that is, the christocentric center of all history

(Oscar Cullmann).[44] Rather, "the end of time" is the constant drawing point to which everything in Paul points: our hope, endurance, sighing, the unredeemed creation, and even the Spirit (Rom. 8:26). Although Paul would not have agreed with Pascal that "Jesus will be in agony until the end of time,"[45] his gospel proclaims both the death of Christ and our death in him "until he comes" (1 Cor. 11:26), because we hope that the reign of death "will be swallowed up by life" (2 Cor. 5:4). The resurrection of Christ remains incomplete until the final redemption of creation and the resurrection of the dead; for until that time it remains "first fruits." Likewise, the Spirit in us remains the Spirit in a mortal body until the final revelation of God's glory.

The Church as the Dawning of the Glory of God

Because the church has an eschatological horizon and is the proleptic manifestation of the kingdom of God in history, it is the beachhead of the new creation and the sign of the new age in the old world that is "passing away" (1 Cor. 7:31). Therefore we cannot identify the church with the kingdom of God or consider it as a supratemporal reality. Paul does not dwell on the preexistent or posthistorical reality of the church, as suggested, for instance, in Eph. 1:4. The vocation of the church does not consist in self-preservation for eternal life but in service to the created world in the sure hope of the world's transformation at the time of God's final triumph. The last judgment is a judgment not only on the world outside the church but also a judgment that will assess the church's faithfulness to its mission in the world (Rom. 14:10; 2 Cor. 5:11; cf. also 1 Pet. 4:17).

Although the church occupies a central place in Paul's thought, that interest is determined by the two foci that define the church's task in the world. Eschatology and Christology are the constituents of Paul's ecclesiology, and the nature of their interrelation determines the character

44. Cullmann, *Christ and Time.*
45. As n. 33 above.

and function of the church. For instance, when eschatology and Christology are conflated, there is the danger of identifying the church with the kingdom of God. When, on the other hand, eschatology and Christology are divorced from each other, an apocalyptic sectarianism displaces the Christ-centered conception of the church. In this case eschatology is so elevated over Christology that fear of the last judgment, religious uncertainty, and a legalistic ethic gain the upper hand. Although the Reformation subordinated the church as the *ecclesia semper reformanda* to God's eschatological judgment, the danger of an individualistic conception of the church has since then often overshadowed the notion of the church as a corporate body. In that case, the church as an aggregate of justified individuals tends to overshadow its corporate character and its eschatological horizon.

Yet we must acknowledge that Paul rarely elaborates a doctrine of the church in his letters. In fact, he inherits the term "church" (*ekklēsia*) from the Christian community at Antioch. Moreover, the concept of the "body of Christ" (*sōma Christou*) rarely occurs in his correspondence. In Romans, for example, the term *ekklēsia* is absent (except in chap. 16), and the motif of "the body of Christ" occurs only in the paraenetic section of Rom. 12:4, 5.

Although the unity of the church is a gift of God's justifying grace (Rom. 5:17-21; cf. 2 Cor. 5:14), this unity is always threatened by unforeseen "contingent situations," not only by the surrounding world outside the walls of the church, but also by the invasion of worldly elements into the church. Dissension, quarreling, factions, pride, jealousy, and immorality (1 Cor. 5:1) all threaten to tear the church apart and divide Christ himself (1 Cor. 1:13). In this context Paul applies a current Hellenistic-Roman metaphor of the body and its members (the *Stoa*) to the church in order to guarantee its health and cohesion.

Because the one body of Christ is a given reality in Christ, Paul never calls for faith in the church or exhorts Christians *to become* the church or the "body of Christ."

Despite its rare occurrence in Paul, the motif of the body of Christ (1 Cor. 12:12–27; Rom. 12:4–5) belongs to a field of interrelated metaphors and images that together express the reality of communal participation of the members in the body of Christ.

Thus it seems as if Paul is experimenting with multiple associations in formulating our new reality in Christ: "oneness" (*heis* [Gal. 3:28]); "the same spirit" (*to auto pneuma,* 1 Cor. 12:9, 11); "one for all" and "one man's act for the many" (*di' henos . . . pantas; henos anthrōpou . . . hoi polloi,* Rom. 5:18, 19); and "in Christ Jesus" (*en Christō Iēsou,* Gal. 3:28; Rom. 8:1). The body metaphor not only gathers together the various aspects of participation in Christ, but also illustrates the notion of the members' mutual interdependence in the life of the church.

Yet there is in Paul a movement away from the metaphorical use of the body motif toward its ontological status (1 Cor. 12:27), so that he can actually call Christ the church (1 Cor. 12:12b). The incorporation motif, which dominates the image of the body of Christ, accentuates both Paul's organic and historical thinking. The motif originates in the Jewish notion of "corporate personality" and embraces a number of components: (1) the one for all; (2) the one in all; and (3) the once for all.

The "once for all" expresses the eschatological-historical event of the death and resurrection of Christ (cf. Rom. 5:15–19; 6:10) that marks the end of the old age and the inauguration of the new age.

The "one for all" describes the death of Christ as the act of God's grace for his people, who henceforth partake of him ("the one in all" and "all in the one"; cf. Rom. 5:12–29; 1 Cor. 15:22). In some contexts the spatial imagery of "in Christ" (1 Cor. 15:22) shifts into the temporal imagery of "with Christ" (Rom. 6:1–8). It permits Paul to emphasize the historical dimension of our life in Christ, because it expresses not only the apocalyptic future of the Christ-event but also its proleptic manifestation in our present existence: "If we have died *with* Christ, we believe that we shall also live *with* him" (Rom. 6:8).

The Ekklēsia

We have seen that the unity of the church and the mutual interdependence of its members is expressed in the body (*sōma*) metaphor. The *ekklēsia* ("church") concept now discloses a different aspect of the church.

1. Whereas Paul himself probably introduced the body metaphor into Christian theology, he inherited the *ekklēsia* concept from the Jewish-Hellenistic church.

2. The body metaphor enables Paul to emphasize special elements that the traditional *ekklēsia* concept does not sufficiently address. Thus the body metaphor is linked to the somatic-ethical character of Christian life as a life *in* the body *for* other bodies *within* "the body of Christ" (1 Cor. 12:14). For although the *ekklēsia* concept contains the idea of "the one assembled people of God," it is not able to stress either the christocentric participation motif or the specific sociological dimensions of unity in the midst of diversity.

3. Therefore, the emphasis on "one" (*hen*) in the metaphor of the body (*sōma*) is absent from the term *ekklēsia*. While the plural for *sōma* is unthinkable, it is regularly used for *ekklēsia* (Rom. 16:4, 16; Gal. 1:2; 1 Cor. 8:18, 19, 23, 24). From this we may conclude that the body metaphor is christocentric, whereas the *ekklēsia* concept has a theocentric thrust.

4. Whereas the body metaphor has important ramifications for the concept of a universal church—since it implies the incorporation of all believers in Christ—the *ekklēsia* concept almost always refers to a local congregation (Rom. 16:1; 1 Cor. 11:18, 22; 14:4, 5, 12, 23, 28) or to a group of congregations (Rom. 16:4, 16; Gal. 1:2, 22; 1 Cor. 4:17; 7:17; 11:16; 16:1). Thus the *ekklēsia* concept stresses both the worshiping activity of the church when it "comes together" (*synerchomai,* 1 Cor. 11:18, 20, 33) and the eschatological character of the people of God, in their "open" access to God's grace (Rom. 5:2). The metaphor of the body, however, expresses more adequately both our participation in Christ and the mutual interdependence of all

the various members of the one body of Christ. Because the glory of God already casts its rays in the church, the church must strive in accordance with its destiny to embody already in this world the freedom and unity of the coming kingdom of God. This brings us back to the problem of coherence and contingency. It appears in this context as the basic tension between the truth of the gospel and the unity of the church. For how can the unity of the church—"the bond of perfect harmony" (Col. 3:14)—be preserved when the church is in conflict with the truth of the gospel?

Thus a conflict can arise between these two poles of Paul's thought. This conflict appears clearly when Paul discusses the tension between freedom and love (1 Corinthians 8–10; Galatians 5; Romans 14–15), a subject frequently addressed in the context of the unity of the church. When Paul admonishes Christians to show forbearance to "weak" brothers (1 Corinthians 8–10; Romans 14–15), is he not sacrificing the truth of the gospel's radical freedom? Is he not reintroducing "the weak and beggarly elemental spirits" (Gal. 4:4, 9)—whether idols, gods, or the law— which the death of Christ has abolished once for all? At what price then does Paul buy the unity of the church at the price of the truth of the gospel?

We must be aware of the fact, however, that Paul operates not only with an ethic of theological principle but also with a situation ethics. He employs them in a contingent manner, because the particularity of every situation must determine what counts as apostasy and what is merely immature faith.

At this point it once more becomes clear that Paul's thought is characterized by the interaction of coherence and contingency. Paul risks the charge of inconsistency because there is no doctrinal principle or yardstick that determines in advance when and where "principle" takes precedence over "situation" or when and where "the truth of the gospel" must prevail over "the unity of the church."

5

The Enigma of the Law and the Struggle between Sin and Death

Within the scope of this book the main themes of Paul's thought could be painted only in broad strokes. In closing I would like briefly to address some specific problems that form an essential part of any sketch of Paul's theology.

THE LAW AMID THE STRUGGLE
BETWEEN THE POWERS

Although I have already addressed the question of Paul's conception of the law in relation to Romans 7 and Galatians 3 (see chapter 3 above), it remains unclear, however, whether the various contingent arguments used by Paul exhibit a clear, coherent view of the law or are simply inconsistent, intuitive, or opportunistic constructs.

The riddle with respect to Paul's understanding of the law is that he describes the law not only as an instrument of God but also as a servant of sin. Thus the question arises: Is the law only a toy at the mercy of opposing powers or does it retain a recognizable identity of its own?

Likewise, one may ask whether there exists a common ground on this issue between Paul and Judaism, so that a meaningful discussion can occur? It seems that Paul's inconsistency is due to Paul's disposition before and after the Damascus experience. On the one hand, Gal. 1:14 and Phil.

3:7 witness to the theme of "joy in the law" (*śimchat hattôra*); on the other hand, he writes, "For no human being will be justified in his sight by works of the law, since through the law comes the knowledge of sin" (Rom. 3:20). Is Paul the convert imposing on Judaism a point of view that amounts to a fatal misunderstanding and misrepresentation of Judaism?[1] Or does Paul's confession of Christ lead him simply to exclude and reject the Jewish understanding of the law?[2] Or shall we say that Paul accuses the Jew of a misguided zeal in attempting to fulfill the law?[3]

It seems to me that Paul has indeed a coherent view of the law. It consists in his radicalization of the Jewish concept of sin. While Judaism associates sin with "the evil impulse" that can only be atoned for through the sacrificial system as ordained by the law, Paul's Christophany led him to a deeper understanding of sin. Only now he recognizes that sinful acts lead to slavery to sin, to a human predicament from which there is "no exit" (cf. John 8:34). The Christophany, which showed that the crucified Messiah was vindicated by God and installed as Lord and as the inaugurator of the new age, convinced Paul that "the holy, just, good and spiritual law" (Rom. 7:12-14) is abused by sin and therefore has itself become a slave to sin. The differentiation between the ontological and ontic function of the law (see chapter 3 above) enables Paul to regard the law not only as a divine instrument, which makes sin accountable to God (Rom. 4:15; 5:20), but also as a servant to sin (Rom. 7:12-14; 6:14; 7:5-8; 1 Cor. 15:56; and so on).

This *ontic* function of the law becomes even clearer when viewed from the perspective of *salvation-history*. The law receives an essentially negative task, that is, to be the instrument that must "augment the trespasses" [(Rom. 5:20); cf. Gal. 3:19: "to specify crimes" (Jerus. Bible)]. In fact, it was God's plan to secure our redemption at the low point of salvation-history, that is, at the place where the law

1. Schoeps, *Paul*, 213ff.
2. Sanders, *Paul and Palestinian Judaism*, 474ff.
3. Bultmann, *Theology of the New Testament* 1:264.

sealed our no-exit plight before God. It was then that God sent Christ "in the fullness of time" (Gal. 4:4) in order "to adopt us as his children" (Gal. 4:5) and to transfer us into the realm of faith and the Spirit (Gal. 3:25; Rom. 8:1-17). Paul expresses his wonder at the mysterious plan of God: "O the depth of the riches and wisdom and knowledge of God! How unsearchable are his judgments and how inscrutable his ways!" (Rom. 11:33).

Paul stresses, therefore, the discontinuous character of the Christ-event as the dawning of a new age, but he does this without surrendering the continuity of God's salvation-historical plan. His new faith perspective enables him to see that the twofold tyranny of sin and the law must give way to the redemptive purpose of God.

In conclusion I would like to address a theme often overlooked in New Testament scholarship, even though it is important for a more adequate understanding of Paul's interpretation of the law. Paul's thesis that Christ is the end as well as the goal of the law (Rom. 10:4) cannot be adequately understood unless we take seriously the nature of Paul's personal encounter with the law. In other words, we must find the appropriate hermeneutical key to unlock Paul's conviction on this point. The aversion of modern New Testament scholarship toward nineteenth-century psychological analyses of Paul's conversion has—since the classical study of W. G. Kümmel[4]—nevertheless led to possible mystifications when it comes to explaining Paul's call. Skepticism reigns whenever the call of Paul is discussed in the light of his former Jewish life. Many scholars seem satisfied with the explanation of Paul's conversion as a "lightning bolt from heaven"! Paul commits himself to Christ "in a flash" and in a "totally unprepared" manner. At stake, however, is not a speculative explanation of the element of surprise in Paul's conversion, but rather the question of what influence his life as a Jew had on this event. How could the Christophany have been so traumatic and radical had it not lit up and answered a hidden quest

---

4. Kümmel, *Römer 7 und die Bekehrung des Paulus.*

in his soul?[5] What actually was the nature of the collision between Paul the Pharisee and Paul the Christian?

The presence of an autobiographical element in Romans 7 cannot be denied. Although the chapter presents a Christian perspective on Jewish life (vv. 4–6) rather than Paul's Christian autobiography (vv. 14–25), it is nevertheless undeniable that only an autobiographical element can explain the vivid confessional cry of verse 24a. Moreover, the personal tone of verses 14–25 seems inexplicable, if not deceptive, if it in fact describes something that was completely alien to Paul's Jewish experience. A deletion of every autobiographical reference in Romans 7 obscures the theological meaning of the text and renders it fruitless for gaining insight into Paul's relationship to Judaism. If we claim that the lordship of Christ simply represents a fully unexpected revelation that has no experiential basis in the former Jewish life of Paul, then it is incomprehensible how and why for him the law is superseded by Christ. For if Paul had been a completely "happy" Jew before he met Christ, his Christian hindsight of his "unhappy" Jewish past in Rom. 7:7-25 would be false and inauthentic, because his statements would lack any foothold in his own experience. If it is claimed that for Paul the lordship of Christ is dogmatically incompatible with the lordship of the Torah,[6] his reflections would constitute only a Christian rear guard struggle against Judaism and would hardly be a product of his experiential conviction. It is unlikely that Paul could have written Rom. 1:18—2:29 without any knowledge of a Jewish awareness of sin and boasting. When he indicts the Jews for transgressing the law and for boasting in spite of their trespasses, he must have experienced this tension within his own Jewish life.

Only on the basis of his personal experience can Paul maintain that Christ not only nullifies the law, because it evokes sin, but also fulfills it, since "love is the fulfillment

5. E. P. Sanders overlooks this problem, but cf. Theissen's criticism of some of Kümmel's theses in *Psychological Aspects,* 177–201.
6. Sanders, *Paul and Palestinian Judaism,* 474ff.

of the law" (Rom. 13:10; cf. Gal 5:14). Therefore, Christians are able to fulfill the righteousness required by the law (Rom. 8:4).

THE DILEMMA OF SIN AND DEATH: EQUAL OR DISPARATE POWERS?

The relationship between sin and death is described by Paul in an apparently ambivalent manner. Sin (*hamartia*) and death (*thanatos*) constitute the most formidable powers of the old age, which in turn determine the function of the law (*nomos*) and flesh (*sarx*) in the world. Sin and death are closely allied and are portrayed as personified powers. Both "rule" over the old age (Rom. 5:12-21); sin is capable of deceiving (Rom. 7:11), and death has a "sting" and a victorious reign (1 Cor. 15:55). Indeed, sin is the procreator of death: "As sin came into the world through one man and death through sin, and so death spread to all because all sinned" (Rom. 5:12). For just as "sin reigned in death" (Rom. 5:21), so "the body of sin" (Rom. 6:6) is a synonym for "this body of death" (Rom. 7:24). The poisonous instrument of death (its "sting") is sin (1 Cor. 15:56), and "the provisions of sin is death" (Rom. 6:23). The alliance between sin and death is indeed deeply entwined: "When the commandment came, sin came to life and I died" (Rom. 7:9-10a).

The question then is this: If sin and death are intertwined and if sin is the progenitor of death as well as its deadly weapon, how can Paul say that sin *has already been* overcome, while death, which is after all the result of sin, remains in effect? For the apostle claims that "the last enemy" to be destroyed is death (1 Cor. 15:26). In view of the twofold thesis that Christ "died to sin once and for all" (Rom. 6:10) and that "death has no longer dominion over him" (Rom. 6:9), the inherent connection between the apocalyptic powers of sin and death becomes a momentous theological problem for Paul. Does Paul, however, give us some clues that enable us to understand this relationship better? How does he explain the continuing reign of death in the suffering and in the cosmic evil of the believer's historical life when Christ is supposed to have procured "a new creation" (Gal. 6:15; 2 Cor. 5:17), that is, a decisive victory over sin and death? Is it Paul's opinion that all cosmic evil can be derived from sin (Rom. 5:12; see above), or does he point to other alternatives? Finally, to what extent is the eschatological destiny of the created order related to this?

It seems to me that Paul's statements on sin and death actually contain a contradiction that cannot be harmonized. This contradiction reflects a problem that has plagued Christians throughout the centuries: the relationship between suffering and evil to sin and death. According to Paul death is "the last enemy" (1 Cor. 15:26), and not until it is destroyed can one speak of God's complete victory. Thus the reign of death in the world intensifies as well the suffering of the church. Although Christians have a share in the reign of Christ, who has conquered death through his resurrection (Rom. 6:9), and although they are human beings "who have been brought from death to life" (Rom. 6:13), death still leaves its poisonous mark on the church in the world as on the world itself. Christians continue to be subject to death (1 Thess. 4:13), and death remains active in "creation's bondage to decay" (Rom. 8:20, 21), that is, in all the groaning and suffering of this world. In agreement with Jewish apocalyptic, Paul nevertheless proclaims that suffering is caused by sin, the sin of Adam, which brought death into the world (Rom. 5:12; see above). This *causal relationship* between sin and death involves Paul in a contradiction that concerns the reign of death as reflected in Christian suffering in the world. If there is a causal connection between sin and death, it is only a logical deduction that Christ's victory over sin brings with it a victory over death. But why then are Christians still subject to death? How can Paul simultaneously conjoin and disjoin the powers of sin and death?

Paul becomes entangled in this contradiction because he is unwilling to grant something that we must acknowledge, that is, that sin and death are to some extent independent powers. Indeed, in human experience suffering caused by sin and suffering caused by death cannot simply be placed on the same level. There is a suffering in the world that cannot be traced back to human sin. Despite this inconsistency in his thought, Paul is nevertheless able to give a more differentiated conception of the matter in some contexts: Christians are already freed from the power of sin (Rom. 6:1-14) and someday *will* be freed from the power of death, when death, "the last enemy" (1 Cor. 15:26), will be destroyed by the final triumph of God.

6

Summary

It has been my intent in this book to argue that Paul's theology is determined by two axioms: the contingent particularity of his hermeneutic and his profound understanding of the coherent structure of the gospel. Therefore Paul should be understood as an interpretive—rather than as a systematic—theologian. The center of Paul's thought not only draws central convictions from the pluriform and various early Christian gospel traditions, but "embodies" them as well in various contextual situations.

Paul's hermeneutical achievement is his ability to connect particularity and universality, pluriformity and unity in such a way that the gospel is not imposed on concrete situations as if it were a fixed "orthodox" system, nor does it become fragmented in incidental, opportunistic, or momentary thoughts.

For this reason Paul's gospel would disintegrate into an abstract system if the interplay between coherence and contingency were overlooked and neglected. For the same reason Paul's gospel would be perverted into an opportunistic structure if one discerned only the contingent character of the gospel without its necessary relation to its coherence.

The coherence-contingency scheme, then, provides a welcome middle ground between the extremes of a purely socio-historical/sociological or rhetorical analysis and a dogmatic imposition of a specific center on Paul's thought. Misinterpretations are apt to obscure the theological truth-claim of Paul's gospel, whether in the form of the dogmatic *loci* of a catechism or as an intricate dialectic of cross and resurrection.[1]

The interplay between coherence and contingency protects the truth-claim of both the "dogmatic" and the "sociological" aspects of Paul's thought because it does not explore the abstruse dialectical notion of interacting theological ideas.[2] Rather it focuses on a quite different kind of dialectic: that between the truth of the gospel and its "incarnational" saving relevance for people's concrete lives and circumstances in the midst of an idolatrous world.

But now the question arises: What precisely constitutes the coherence of Paul's gospel?

My adoption of the term "coherence" focuses on the fluid and flexible structure of Paul's thought. Rather than connotating a fixed core and a specific center or particular symbol, it points to a field of meaning—a network of symbolic relations that nourishes Paul's thought—something analogous to the coherent field of interlocking circles on the Olympic logo. This field of meaning is determined by the apocalyptic coordinates of Paul's "linguistic world," so that apocalyptic defines the network of the symbolic relations in Paul's thought.

An important distinction must be made, however, between Paul's fundamental symbolic structure and its diverse linguistic expressions. Paul's evangelical "center" should not be identified with one of its soteriological metaphors, for instance, "the righteousness of God," "justification," "redemption," "reconciliation," or "being in Christ." Rather they are "metaphors of relevance," that is, they are words

---

1. Cf. for instance the characterization of death and life as a dialectic *sub contrario* notion in Käsemann.

2. Cf. for instance the above mentioned *sub contrario* notion in Käsemann or Barth's thesis of "The Infinite Qualitative Distinction between Time and Eternity."

on target, appropriate for the specific situation the gospel proclamation encounters.

The apocalyptic field of meaning, determined and modified by the Christ-event, constitutes the decisive coherent center of Paul's thought. A crucified Jesus—vindicated and raised by God—convinced Paul of the truth of Jesus' status as Messiah and Son of God. And since resurrection-speech for a Pharisee like Paul was intelligible only in terms of apocalyptic language, this language is therefore not simply an expression of a contingent symbolism, but represents the coherent center of Paul's thought.

The characterization of Paul's thought as the apocalyptic interpretation of the Christ-event necessitates a revision of a common and widely accepted conception of Paul's theology in at least two regards:

1. Paul's theology is marked by its *theocentric* character. Contrary to a common consensus that posits a christocentric scheme of promise and fulfillment, Paul refuses to spiritualize the promises of the Old Testament. His hope in a glorified creation makes it necessary for him to give theocentric ideas a place of priority over his christological thought, because God continues to be faithful to his promises for his world. The focal point of Paul's thought is therefore theocentric because it longs for the public manifestation of God's reign and triumph.

In this context it strikes us how important the vocabulary of "God's glory" (*doxa*) and of "the hope" (*elpis*) is to Paul. The meaning of hope is in Paul not simply restricted to a disposition inherent in faith (cf. R. Bultmann, *elpis, TDNT*), but rather implies a specific objective content, that is, the "glory [*doxa*] of the coming aeon" (Rom. 5:2; 8:18; cf. 8:17, 21, 30; Phil. 2:11; cf. also Rom. 8:23: "the redemption of our body"; 1 Thess. 1:10: "to wait for his Son from heaven"; Rom. 5:1: "cosmic" peace; Gal. 5:5: "we wait for the hope of righteousness"). Thus the resurrection of Christ and his present glory do not represent the climax of salvation history—as in the Gospel of John; rather the climax of salvation-history is constituted by the coming glory of God, in whose name Christ exercises his reign (Phil. 2:11).

2. Because Paul makes a significant distinction between the power of sin and the power of death, and regards the latter as a power that is still operative until the public manifestation of God's coming triumph, it opens up new possibilities for Christian reflection to view suffering, evil, and death from a perspective of hope. For the promise of God's final triumph over the power of death provides us with a horizon of hope, which resists every form of masochism and every conception of the love of God as impotence.

Moreover, the notion of a definitive victory of God over the power of death stimulates a contingent ethic of solidarity, not only because both Christians and the world are still subject to the power of death, but also because the last judgment will demand from Christians a final accountability of their stewardship over God's creation and of the manner in which they have exercised their solidarity with the world.

And finally a nonacademic postscript: J. S. Bach was perhaps the most prominent interpreter of Paul. In contrast to the present triumph of the anthropological and sociological interpretation of Paul's theology, Bach's music, not only his choral preludes and cantatas, but especially his great organ works, directs the listener to the transcendent dimensions of the majesty of God. And so Bach intuited and discerned already in his time that the glorification of the almighty God—and not anthropology or social history—constitutes the true point of departure for understanding Paul's theology.

Paul the Theologian
Major Motifs
in Pauline Theology[1]

I. METHODOLOGICAL CONSIDERATIONS

A. There is a tendency in recent Pauline scholarship to move away from Paul the theologian, that is, from an inquiry into Paul's theological center and the theological claims of his texts to a psychological and sociological description of Paul. However fruitful the concentration on the descriptive aspects of Paul's person and world is, it entails the danger of displacing the theological claims of the Pauline texts for subtextual concerns. With respect to Paul, we are apt to forget Rudolf Bultmann's insightful summary that the task of New Testament theology is not the "reconstruction of past history" but rather the "interpretation of the New Testament writings"; thus "reconstruction stands in the service of the interpretation of the New Testament under the presupposition that they have something to say to the present."[2]

Recent Pauline scholarship has indeed demonstrated that the confidence of an earlier generation to establish the center of Paul's thought (cf. William Wrede; Albert Schweitzer) rested on shaky ground and that a closer analysis of the

1. This article is reprinted by permission from *Interpretation, 43,* (1989): 352–65.
2. *Theology of the New Testament* (New York: Charles Scribner's Sons, 1955), 2:251.

117

phenomenological aspects of Paul's thought is a necessary condition for understanding the apostle. However, an even more urgent task awaits us in the light of Bultmann's understanding of what constitutes a New Testament theology: an evaluation of the truth-claims of the Pauline text rather than simply the exploration of their utility for descriptive purposes. Paul's text does not refer primarily to the social history of his world or to the psychodynamics of his person but rather to God's redemptive action in Christ for faith.

B. The truth-claim of Paul's gospel necessitates an inquiry into the center of his thought, but it is also clear how difficult such an inquiry is. Paul did not write a "dogmatics in outline" or philosophical letter-essays (e.g., Seneca), and he did not leave us with an essay on "How I changed my mind," or delineate his thought-patterns in a logical sequential manner. Moreover, Paul is not a thinker whose originality and creativity can be found in his doctrinal architecture or in soliloquies and meditations in the manner of Marcus Aurelius (*"Eis Heauton"*). All we possess from him are seven authentic letters—written at different times and for widely different occasions. A series of such occasional letters makes it very difficult to posit the center of their author's thought.

Paul is essentially an *interpreter* of the gospel: He interprets the tradition which he inherited from the church at Antioch after his conversion and call to the apostolate. The thought of an interpreter is necessarily different from that of a speculative thinker, because the freedom of an interpreter's thought is delimited by the tradition in which he stands and which he interprets.

Furthermore, the difficulty of an inquiry into the center of Paul's thought is increased by the fact that the interpreter of Paul cannot be satisfied with a "fragmented Paul," with a few "central" texts drawn from a selection of his letters. Rather the interpreter must embrace "the whole Paul," Paul as represented by the whole of his authentic letters.

Finally, when we characterize Paul as a *theologian,* we expect his thought to be consistent and coherent; for unless it is coherent, its intelligibility is in doubt, and its relevance cannot be demonstrated. In that case Paul's thought falls apart into a series of trivial, incidental assertions and must be assigned to the archeological depository.

C. In the light of these obstacles, two possibilities suggest themselves: One either denies the existence of a coherent center altogether or one locates it somewhere other than in Paul's theology. However, in both instances the surface meaning of the text becomes a means for another purpose. In the latter instance the text becomes a means for locating Paul's center in a subtextual layer or stratum, for instance, in his psyche or in his intuition or in his (prelinguistic) convictions.[3] In the first instance the text becomes a means for tracing Paul's social world and/or its impact on his symbolic system[4] or for delineating the nature of his rhetoric.

D. We must be aware of the fact that the possibility of establishing the center of Paul's thought has become the subject of much doubt in recent Pauline scholarship. For instance, Hendrikus Boers states that the identification of a center which "integrates the diversity of the apostle's thinking into a coherent whole is the most fundamental problem in Pauline interpretation,"[5] while Hans Hübner concludes that "the theme of contradictions in Paul" requires an urgent solution.[6] Skepticism with regard to the issue of a coherent center is often accompanied by an outright denial of its presence in Paul. Recent scholarship has essentially proposed four solutions to the problem:

(1) Paul is on the whole coherent, but he is not systematic.[7]

3. Daniel Patte, *Paul's Faith and the Power of the Gospel* (Philadelphia: Fortress Press, 1983).
4. Wayne Meeks, *The First Urban Christians* (New Haven: Yale University Press, 1983); Norman Petersen, *Rediscovering Paul: Philemon and the Sociology of Paul's Narrative World* (Philadelphia: Fortress Press, 1985).
5. Proposal for SBL Meeting, Atlanta, 1986, p. 2.
6. "Methodologie und Theologie: Zu neuen methodischen Ausätzen in der Paulusforschung," *KuD* 33 (1987): 150–75.
7. E. P. Sanders, *Paul and Palestinian Judaism* (Philadelphia: Fortress Press, 1977) and *Paul, the Law, and the Jewish People* (Philadelphia: Fortress Press, 1983).

(2) Paul is incoherent; there is no coherent center in Paul.[8]
(3) Paul's developmental theological journey explains his contradictory thoughts (Hübner, among others).
(4) Paul's coherent center must be located in his psyche (Gerd Theissen).

Sanders insists that in Paul's conviction, reason, and argument conflict, so that his arguments often contradict his basic conviction. Although Sanders considers Paul to be a coherent thinker, he is, according to Sanders, more often than not unconvincing.
Räisänen concludes:

> It is a fundamental mistake of much Pauline exegesis in this century to have portrayed Paul as the "prince of thinkers" and the Christian "theologian par excellence." . . . He is quite capable of putting forward a statement which logically contradicts the previous one when trying to make a different point or, rather, struggling with a different problem. . . . Christian theology should have fastened on Paul's intuition. . . . Instead, especially in Protestantism, the rationalizations Paul contrived in support of his intuition came to be seen as his actual invaluable accomplishment. I propose that we return to stress the intuition.[9]

Whereas these scholars detect a cleavage between the text of the letters and Paul's real intent, proponents of a development-theory of Paul's thought attribute the cleavage and Paul's contradictions to his evolving theological development, to Paul's progressive theological journey from First Thessalonians to Romans and/or Ephesians.

In this context the remarkable book of Gerd Theissen should be mentioned.[10] Theissen does not focus on contradictions in Paul's thought but rather gives us a balanced and integrated picture of that thought. In contrast to earlier

8. H. Räisänen, *Paul and the Law* (Philadelphia: Fortress Press, 1986); *The Torah and Christ* (Helsinki: The Finnish Exegetical Society, 1986).
9. *Paul and the Law*, 266–69.
10. *Psychological Aspects of Paul's Theology* (Philadelphia: Fortress Press, 1987).

psychological analyses of Paul's soul (for instance—in the footsteps of Friedrich W. Nietzsche—R. L. Rubinstein's "My Brother Paul";[11] cf. also Paul Wernle,[12] Heinrich Weinel[13]), Theissen combines text-analysis and tradition-analysis with psychological analysis in a fruitful manner. Yet even here the question arises whether Theissen's psychoanalytical probes into Paul do not ultimately suffocate the question of the truth-claims of the Pauline texts.

E. The feasibility of a subtextual center of Paul's thought will be my focus here, since Paul the theologian is the topic of this essay. But why a subtextual center? Its possibility is enhanced in the light of a widespread consensus that Paul's coherent center cannot be identified with any one concept of Paul's letters. The time is past when a preferred key term of Paul is played off against others *or* when the preferred term is simply imposed on "the whole Paul" (i.e., on the totality of Paul's letters). For instance, the "Lutheran" method of equating the center of Paul with the concept of justification by faith is—notwithstanding its profundity—based on a "fragmented" reading of Paul.

Thus, if we grant that the coherent center of Paul can be discerned only in the substratum of the text, its claim of unlocking the center of Paul's thought still is subject to a fundamental methodological criterion, that is, the distance or proximity of the discerned center to the text of the letters. For unless the text itself remains the ultimate arbiter for establishing the validity of Paul's coherent center, we fall victim to speculations, ideologies, and arbitrary prejudgments and are no longer engaged in the proper business of exegesis.

F. In this context my own previous construal of the coherent center of Paul's thought is subject to a criticism similar to the one which can be directed against those scholars who locate the center in the substratum of the

11. *My Brother Paul* (New York: Harper & Row, 1972).
12. *Die Anfänge unserer Religion,* 2d ed. (Tübingen: J. C. B. Mohr [Paul Siebeck], 1904).
13. *Biblische Theologie des Neuen Testaments: Die Religion Jesu und des Urchristentums* (Tübingen: J. C. B. Mohr [Paul Siebeck], 1911).

text—whether in a cleavage between Paul's convictions (or intuition) and their expressions or in his contradictory utterances—for I myself also located this center in a layer underneath the text.[14]

The coherence-contingency model which I proposed as a way to explicate the nature of Paul's hermeneutic attempts to maintain both the coherence or basic constant theological structure of Paul's thought and the contingency or situational particularity and diversity of its various expressions. I argued that the model requires a clarification of at least two basic issues: (1) the precise delineation of the *interaction* between coherence and contingency and (2) the nature of the *coherence* of Paul's gospel.[15]

The interaction between coherence and contingency: In comparing Paul's hermeneutic with post-Pauline construals of the interaction between coherence and contingency, a remarkable difference can be observed. For instance, in the Pastoral Epistles, *the confluence* in Paul between coherence and contingency is broken apart by *a bifurcation* of a fixed "timeless" coherence ("the deposit of truth" [*paratheke,* 1 Tim. 6:20; 2 Tim. 1:14]; "sound doctrine" [*hygiainousa didaskalia,* 1 Tim. 1:10; 2 Tim. 4:13]) and a contingency, which the author does not consider worthy of accurate description or serious engagement. In other words, the dialogical character of Paul's hermeneutic is here displaced by imposition, monologue, and moral vilification.

A similar move might be seen in the Jewish interpretation of Torah in *halakah* and in the Christian orthodox application of the creed. Here the coherence-contingency model lacks the fluidity of Paul's hermeneutic; the hermeneutic is not engaged in an interpenetration between normative principles and cases but rather consists in a casuistic application of established principles.

The nature of the coherence of Paul's gospel: I suggested that that coherence is constituted by the range of Paul's

14. J. Christiaan Beker, *Paul the Apostle* (Philadelphia: Fortress Press, 1984), 15–18.

15. J. Christiaan Beker, "Paul's Theology: Consistent or Inconsistent," *NTS* 34 (1988): 368–71.

abiding theological convictions and comprises a network of symbolic relations, which are held together by Paul's apocalyptic interpretation of the Christ-event, the *apokalypsis Iesou Christou* (Gal. 1:12; cf. 1:16; 2:2). Apocalyptic motifs form the substratum of Paul's thought, because apocalyptic served as the filter, context, and grammar for his understanding of the Christ-event.

Thus, instead of equating Paul's center with one particular symbol or metaphor (such as justification, reconciliation, freedom, being in Christ), the coherence or symbolic structure of Paul's thought is located in a substratum of the text and contains the totality of the contingent symbols, which he employs in his letters.

G. However, the preceding explication of my coherence-contingency model contains some problematic features.

First, the distinction between the two constituent elements of the model—the coherent and contingent—presupposes clearly defined boundaries between the abiding/constant elements of the gospel ("coherence") and its variable elements ("contingency"). Yet, if the interaction between coherence and contingency in Paul's letters deviates sharply from its later usage, as I suggested above, a clear distinction between these two constituent elements is difficult to maintain. Moreover, it is precisely Paul's dialogical manner of doing theology which militates against the possibility of a precise delineation of these boundaries.

Second, in my proposal the concept "coherence" carries a double and thus seemingly an ambivalent meaning. "Coherence" means primarily "the quality of being logically integrated, consistent, and intelligible (*Webster*). Accordingly, a coherence-theory of truth defines truth "more in terms of logical, consistent statement than in terms of any truth-claim" (*Encyclopedia of Philosophy*). Therefore "coherence" must primarily refer to the integration of Paul's basic convictions with the demands of the contingent situation, that is, to his hermeneutic ability in achieving a confluence and interpenetration of his basic convictions and the contingent situations. In other words, coherence means here the natural *result* of Paul's hermeneutical activity and is not a structure prior to it.

However, in my proposal I use "coherence" primarily with respect to the truth-claim of Paul's gospel, that is, with reference to the range of Paul's abiding theological convictions. Thus, since the boundaries of what constitutes coherence cannot be clearly determined in Paul and since, moreover, I did not clearly delineate the double meaning of coherence, the coherence-contingency model seems deficient and incapable to establish the center of Paul's thought.

H. In the light of this critique of my previous proposal, it is necessary to clarify my position and distinguish it from the alternative proposals of the scholars I have discussed above. The problems inherent in my coherence-contingency model do not pertain to its uselessness but to my deficient explication of it. In fact, my objections may serve to clarify the *proprium* of Paul's thought and the texture of his hermeneutic.

(1) The fact that the boundaries of "the coherent" cannot be clearly determined points to the *basic fluidity* between Paul's basic convictions and their interaction with contingent situations. The fluidity opens up a wide range of hermeneutical possibilities, and permits Paul to enter into an open dialogue with his various audiences. Far from *imposing* his basic convictions on his audience, Paul's hermeneutical fluidity produces in most cases a "fusion of horizons" between the apostle and his interrogatories (however, cf. 1 Corinthians 15 below). Thus the fluid boundaries between convictions and contingency belong to the essence of Paul's hermeneutic.

(2) The twofold meaning of the concept "coherence" fosters Paul's hermeneutical fluidity as well. It alerts us to the necessary *distinction* in Paul's hermeneutic between (a) his fundamental convictions (coherence as "theological base") and (b) his success or failure in achieving an integration between his convictions and the contingent situations which he faces (coherence as "consistency").

(3) Finally, because Paul's theological base is situated in a subtextual location, the coherence of his thought cannot be simply lifted from the text of the letters, since the text only reveals the particular intertwining and reciprocity of coherence and contingency, that is, the outcome of their hermeneutical interaction. Thus, the subtextual location of "the coherent" also serves Paul's hermeneutic fluidity, because it enables him to operate with a plurality of theological metaphors according to their contextual suitability rather than be limited to a particular idea or doctrinal "core," that is, to a fixed, nonpliable bedrock.

I. In brief, although there is widespread agreement that Paul's coherent center cannot be identified with any one metaphor of his letters and must be located underneath the text of his letters (cf. above), the crucial issue is whether this subtextual level satisfies the methodological criterion I mentioned above, that is, its distance or proximity to the text of Paul's letters. For unless the discerned coherent center becomes transparent in the text of the letters, it cannot qualify as the key that unlocks Paul's thought. Therefore, I contend that Paul's center cannot be located in his psyche or in convictions which are not formulated in language or in his intuition or in a speculative theory of his theological development, but must be located in the apocalyptic substratum of his thought, which as the filter for his Christian convictions becomes manifest in the text of his letters.

II. SOME MAJOR MOTIFS

In this section I will limit myself essentially to an interpretation of three text-units representative of some basic motifs of Paul's theology: 1 Corinthians 15 (along with Rom. 8:17-30); Philippians 3:4-11; and Romans 9–11. These texts clarify, in conjunction with the foregoing discussion, three interrelated issues of Paul's thought: (a) the *interaction* of the coherent center with contingent situations; (b) the *relation* of specific symbols/motifs in his letters to the coherent center, that is, the relation of the text to its

subtextual center; (c) the contradictory and/or developmental character of Paul's thought.

First Corinthians 15 (along with Rom. 8:17-30):   First Corinthians 15 evokes two interrelated questions: (a) How
do coherence and contingency interact here, and (b) what
constitutes Paul's coherent center? These questions point
not only to the *specificity* of Paul's coherent center but also
to its uneasy relation to contingent situations, at least in 1
Corinthians 15. The interaction between coherence and
contingency becomes problematic in 1 Corinthians 15, because Paul seems simply to impose his apocalyptic coherent
center on the nonapocalyptic worldview of the Corinthians. Although Paul's argument in 1 Corinthians 15 is consistent within the framework of his thought, its
effectiveness and persuasiveness with respect to the worldview of the Corinthians is doubtful.

The Corinthians do not inhabit an apocalyptic worldview. Their gentile worldview is determined by a Hellenistic cosmology, which thinks only in spatial-vertical
categories rather than in the temporal-historical categories
of apocalyptic thought. Why then does Paul, "the apostle
to the *Gentiles*" (Rom. 11:13), who claims to "have become
all things to all men" (1 Cor. 9:22), insist that the truth of
the gospel for these Gentiles in Corinth depends on their
acceptance of a particularist Jewish apocalyptic ideology?

Paul's theology of hope in 1 Corinthians 15 constitutes
the key and climax of the letter. (The *peri*-clauses which
dominate the discussion from 7:11 to 16:1 are interrupted
at 15:1, indicating that in 1 Cor. 15 Paul puts forth his
fundamental theological position, which undergirds directly or indirectly his answers to all the Corinthian in-
quiries.) Over against the Corinthians' claim to be
"spiritually fulfilled selves," who equate the blessings of
Christ with the immediate perfection of life—a perfection
which lifts them above history and frees them from entanglement with the burdens of life in this world—Paul
argues that their spiritual misunderstanding of the death
and resurrection of Christ leads them to a disdain of both

the *temporality* and *physicality* of their lives in history. Therefore, he proclaims that the resurrection of Christ is not the
end of history but rather its promise. Christ is *"the first
fruits* of those who have fallen asleep" (v. 20); and this
promise will not be fulfilled until "the last enemy," death,
is destroyed (v. 26). Only at that time "the Son himself
will also be subjected to him who put all things under him,
that God may be everything to all things" (v. 28; my
translation). This christological understanding affects both
the religious and ethical life of the Corinthians. In contrast
to their boast of religious perfection and ethical self-suf-
ficiency, the *promise* of the resurrection of the dead cautions
them that their lives cannot authenticate themselves but
rather will be authenticated by God in the eschatological
hour. This means that a responsible life in the body, which
issues forth in caring for other bodies in "the body of
Christ," is the criterion for their authentication, as Paul
points out in 1 Corinthians 12–14 (cf. also 15:58). Only at
the hour of the apocalyptic resurrection of the dead, only
when God will be "everything to all things" (v. 28), only
then "shall come to pass the saying that is written 'Death
is swallowed up in victory' " (vv. 54, 55). Indeed, when
Christ is conceived as the total "fullness of God" (Col.
1:19) rather than as "the first fruits" (1 Cor. 15:23) of God's
coming glory, Paul's Christology is distorted; and when a
realized eschatology neglects the meaning of the Spirit as
"first fruits" and divorces the Spirit from its proper location
in the historical world of the body, Paul's anthropology is
perverted. Thus, the apocalyptic matrix of Paul's coherent
center signifies that the fulfillment of God's redemptive
plan for his creation, that is, "the fullness of God," is not
to be equated with the finality of Christ.

The apocalyptic texture of Paul's coherent center in 1
Corinthians 15 shows that—far from considering the apocalyptic worldview a husk or a purely contingent symbol—
it constitutes the master-symbol for the interpretation of
the gospel.

Thus we conclude that:

(1) First Corinthians 15 marks Paul's theology as basically a theology of hope, which resists both a realized eschatology and an exclusive christocentric interpretation of his theology. First Corinthians 15 also shows that a covenantal view of Paul's thought, centered in the question "how to get in and stay in," that is, on the sociological issue of the relation of Jew and Gentile in the church, has a too narrow focus. Paul's coherent center is apocalyptic in the sense that it embraces the *cosmic coordinates* of God's purpose in creation and redemption, that is, it centers in the hope of the ultimate transformation of God's whole created order.

(2) First Corinthians 15 demonstrates the *specificity* of Paul's gospel and its hermeneutical implications, because in Corinth Paul does not compromise—for the sake of missionary success—the central conviction of his gospel, that is, the inseparable relation between the resurrection of Christ and the future resurrection of the dead. Paul's argument, indeed, demonstrates that the specificity of Paul's coherent center is constituted by his apocalyptic interpretation of the Christ-event, for its presence determines for him the truth or distortion of the gospel as a whole.

(3) First Corinthians 15 also shows that the usually intricate confluence and interaction between coherence and contingency in Paul can break apart so that an apparent *collision* between coherence and contingency occurs. This indicates either a betrayal of Paul's claim, "I have become all things to all men, that I might by all means save some" (1 Cor. 9:22), or his unswerving conviction about the pivotal importance of the future resurrection of the dead for the truth of the gospel.

> *Romans 8:17-30:* Although the interaction between the coherent center and the contingent situation in Romans 8:17-30 differs considerably from that in I Corinthians 15— not in the least because Paul develops in Romans 8 in a seemingly noncontingent manner the relation of the church to the world—the apocalyptic focus of Paul's coherent center is again very clear. It is here dominated by the concept "glory" (vs. 17, 18, 21, 30), whereas I Corinthians 15—

due to the contingent situation in Corinth—focuses on the key term "resurrection." Although both "glory" and "resurrection" are constitutive of Paul's coherent center, "glory" serves in Romans 8 to relate the apocalyptic horizon of Paul's thought to the created order—an emphasis less explicit in I Corinthians 15. In other words, the apocalyptic hope of the gospel expects not merely the transformation of Christians in the future resurrection of the dead (I Cor. 15) but also the transformation of God's total created order, so that at the time of "the *apokalypsis* (revealing) of the sons of God" (v. 19) "the creation itself will be set free from its bondage to decay and obtain the freedom of the glory of the children of God" (v. 21).[16]

Philippians 3:4-11: Whereas 1 Corinthians and Romans 8 point to the coherent center on Paul's thought in its interaction with (more or less clear) contingent situations, Phil. 3:4-11 directs our attention to the relation of specific symbols to Paul's coherent center, that is, to the relation of the text to its subtextual center. The key term in Phil. 3:4-11, "righteousness" (*dikaiosynē*), shows that this symbol, along with its cognate "to rightwise" (*dikaioō*), marks (a) Paul's *original* hermeneutic of the Christ-event, (b) the *anticipatory* character of the symbol, and (c) its *contingent* character.

The symbols, "the righteousness of God" and "to rightwise," mark Paul's original hermeneutic of the Christ-event, "original" in order of time rather than in order of importance. This apocalyptic symbol constitutes the linguistic home of Paul's conversion experience, because it was the language by which he appropriated the Christophany and broke with his Pharisaic past: "as to the law a Pharisee, as to zeal a persecutor of the church, as to righteousness under the law blameless" (Phil. 3:5-6). Since for Paul, the Jew, the Torah was the sole means to obtain righteousness and life, his encounter with the risen Christ produced a traumatic collision: The inseparable connection

---

16. Cf. S. J. Kraftchick, "Creation Themes in Pauline Literature," *Ex Auditu* 3 (1987): 72–87.

between the Torah and righteousness was severed; henceforth righteousness is "apart from the law" (Rom. 3:21),
"Christ is the end of the law" (Rom. 10:4; cf. Gal. 2:21)
or in the words of Phil. 3:8b-11:

> For his [Christ's] sake I have suffered the loss of all things,
> and count them as refuse, in order that I may gain Christ
> and be found in him, not having a righteousness of my
> own, based on law, but that which is through faith in
> Christ, the righteousness of God that depends on faith; that
> I may know him and the power of his resurrection, and
> may share his sufferings, becoming like him in his death,
> that if possible I may attain the resurrection from among
> the dead. (My translation)

Philippians 3:8-11 demonstrates as well the anticipatory
meaning of "the righteousness of God," because the present
knowledge of Christ (i.e., the knowledge of God's gift of
righteousness in Christ) looks forward to the final goal,
the resurrection from among the dead (v. 11). In Paul's
words:

> Not that I have already obtained this or am already perfect;
> but I press on to make it my own, because Jesus Christ
> has made me his own—forgetting what lies behind and
> straining forward to what lies ahead, I press on toward the
> goal of the prize of the call from above of God in Christ
> Jesus." (Vv. 12–14, my translation)

Thus the gift of God's righteousness in Christ is the
foundation of Paul's hope for "perfection" (v. 12, i.e., for
"the resurrection of the dead," v. 11), just as in Rom. 5:1-
2 and Rom. 8:30 "our hope of sharing the glory of God"
and our glorification are based on our prior justification.

"Righteousness" and "justification" are, along with the
other symbols of Paul's soteriology, such as "reconciliation," "being in Christ," "freedom," "wisdom," contingent
symbols which all participate in the apocalyptic framework
of Paul's coherent center.

Thus when Käsemann identifies the theme of justification as the central theme of Paul's thought,[17] he is in error,

17. Ernst Käsemann, "The Spirit and the Letter" in *Perspectives on Paul*
(Philadelphia: Fortress Press, 1971), 164.

because justification is a contingent symbol and Paul's sub-textual coherent center must be distinguished from the variety of contingent symbols he employs in the text of his letters.[18] No such contingent symbol employed in accordance with its appropriateness to the demands of a contingent situation can be identified as the central theme of Paul's thought. Thus the interface between the coherent center and its contingent symbols resembles a strategic command center that dispatches the appropriate material according to the needs of the situation in the battle zone. In this way, the coherent center not only comprises all the symbols that are juxtaposed to each other in Paul's letters but also dominates their interpretation. Consequently all these symbols have an anticipatory meaning, because they point to the Christ-event as the proleptic fulfillment of God's final glory and triumph.

In brief, whereas 1 Corinthians 15 and Romans 8 clearly are defined by Paul's coherent center, and show its (occasionally conflictual) interaction with the demands of the contingent situation, texts such as Phil. 3:4-11 demonstrate that symbols like righteousness are, along with the other traditional symbols in Paul's letters, contingent symbols which are not only interrelated but also are related to a coherent center, which gives them their apocalyptic texture and meaning.

Romans 9-11: At this juncture the question arises whether Paul is consistent in his argumentation, that is, whether or not the encounter between coherent center and contingent demands reveals basic contradictions. For instance, Paul conducts an argument in Romans 9-11 which not only contains contradictory features but also seems to conflict with statements he makes elsewhere. It remains unclear, for instance, what Paul means by "Israel" and what the nature of its priority is, an issue which belongs to the basic theme of the letter (1:16; cf. 3:1-3).

18. I will not discuss here the developmental theory of Paul's thought. It also detects inconsistencies and contradictions in Paul, but attempts to account for them by tracing an evolutionary trajectory in Paul's thought.

Paul seems to experiment with several ideas, which are mutually exclusive: In Rom. 9:8 he defines Israel in contrast to "the children of the flesh," that is, ethnic Israel, as "the children of the promise," that is, as the spiritual Israel (cf. Gal. 4:29, where the child of the promise, v. 23, is defined as "the child born according to the Spirit," v. 29). However, in 9:27 he speaks about Israel as "the remnant" or "the seed" (cf. 11:5, 7), that is, in terms of an offshoot from ethnic Israel. And at last a final solution to the problem dawns with the revelation of the "mystery" in 11:25, where he states that "*all Israel* will be saved" (11:26) in the apocalyptic consummation.

Although this last claim applies the apocalyptic thrust of Paul's coherent center to Israel, according to which Israel's priority in salvation-history (11:29) will be confirmed by its eschatological destiny, it contradicts Paul's earlier definitions of Israel. In fact, how can Paul assert Israel's "partial" hardening in 11:25 after claiming Israel's "complete" hardening in 9:22-23 (cf. also 11:7-10)? Here "the vessels of wrath *have been* prepared for destruction" (perfect tense: *katertismena*)—a reference to both Pharaoh's and Israel's destiny. Moreover, the nature of Israel's priority remains unclear: Is the salvation of all of Israel (11:26) dependent on its positive response to Christ (v. 22), on its absorption into the church as the new Israel, *or* is its salvation solely due to God's apocalyptic intervention, which safeguards Israel's integrity as a covenant-people?

The argument in Rom. 9:30—10:13 is again replete with obstacles. Although throughout his letters Paul is negative toward Israel's law, the specific reason for his negativity in 9:30—10:13 is difficult to grasp. E. P. Sanders, for instance, queries with respect to 9:30: "Precisely what is Israel's fault? That they did not reach righteousness by the law, or that they did not succeed in fulfilling the law?"[19] Indeed, if Paul argues that Israel did not succeed in fulfilling the law, because "they did not pursue it through faith, but as if it were based on works" (v. 32), one wonders what

19. *Paul, the Law, and the Jewish People*, 36.

Israel was supposed to have done before the coming of Christ, since the Torah and its *mizwot* ("works") form an inseparable unity in Judaism? How then can Paul argue that Israel did not "attain to the *law*" (v. 31)?

The christological context of the passage suggests that Paul actually means " '*did not attain*' the righteousness through faith in Christ," for Paul is convinced that "the only ground of salvation is faith in Christ, which is available to all without distinction (10:11-13) and which excludes the law as a way to 'righteousness.' "[20] Romans 10:4 supports this interpretation, because in the context of 10:4-13 it can only mean, "Christ is the *end* of the law."

In fact, the unceasing debate whether *telos* in Rom. 10:4 means "goal" or "end" demonstrates the difficulty of maintaining a consistent interpretation of the law in Paul's thought. We are constantly tempted to harmonize the variety of Paul's statements about the law, whereas we fail to observe the various contextual settings of his arguments. Many texts (for instance, Rom. 2:12; 3:21, 31; 8:4; 13:10 and Gal. 5:14) point to Christ as the "goal" or fulfillment of the law, whereas other texts (for instance, Gal. 2:19; 3:12, 13, 22, 23-24; Rom. 6:15; 7:4; 10:4-10) emphasize that Christ is "the end of the law."

However, instead of charging Paul with outright contradictions and fickleness of thought, we should pay close attention to argumentative sequence and to the variety of contingent situations, which determine the particularity of Paul's argumentative strategies. Moreover we must be aware that a theocentric Christology and not the Torah is the proper topic of Paul's theology. As Westerholm puts it: "Only faith in a crucified Messiah forced Paul to explain why the law had not led to life. . . . It is because Paul believes the coming of the new covenant implies the inadequacy of the old that he characterizes the one as resting on divine grace, the other on human works."[21]

20. *Paul, the Law, and the Jewish People*, 42.
21. S. Westerholm, *Israel's Law and the Church's Faith* (Grand Rapids, Mich.: William B. Eerdmans, 1988), 163.

Thus the Christophany before Damascus results in an anthropology that becomes an essential part of Paul's coherent center. The verdict "all are under the power of sin" (Rom. 3:9) is not to be dismissed to the periphery of Paul's thought, as Sanders[22] and Räisänen[23] think but rather forms the indispensable presupposition of the coherent center of Paul's thought. His emphasis on the universal power of sin, which distances his thought from Judaism, enables him to construct a narrative of sin's strategy and cunning. Romans 1:18-32, in conjunction with Rom. 7:7-25, shows how sin's strategy aims at deception and illusion. It creates in us the illusion of freedom and dominion, of permanent choice and a permanent lordship over sin. This self-deception is due to sin's cunning, because we forget that we have moved from a position where sin was the result of transgression to a state of affairs where we are subjugated by sin. Thus sin has become a new lordship, an apocalyptic power which rules and overrules us and which makes the law impotent for salvation.

III. CONCLUSION

A. Paul's thought contains a coherent center, which is located on a subtextual level. We must therefore avoid the error of locating the center in one of the contingent symbols of the text. Thus with respect to Paul's success or failure in integrating in a consistent, noncontradictory manner his coherent center with its contingent demands, I would argue that Paul's coherent center constitutes a distinct but fluid center, which is able to display itself in a variety of arguments according to the various argumentative needs of the hour (Phil. 3:4-11). Although contradictions occasionally occur, it is a mistake to simply list "contradictions" in Paul's thought without regard for the particularity of his contextual argument.

B. The subtextual location of the coherent center fosters the fluidity of Paul's hermeneutic and its applicability to a wide variety of contingent situations.

22. *Paul, the Law, and the Jewish People*, 35–36.
23. *Paul and the Law*, 107–9.

C. Paul's coherent center has an apocalyptic matrix and pattern, which is decisively modified by the Christophany on the Damascus road.

D. The risks involved in all hermeneutical enterprises involve Paul occasionally in contradictory statements and in misperceptions of the rhetorical situation (Romans 9–11); and sometimes he simply imposes the specificity of his gospel on contingent situations, which seem to require a different translation of the gospel (1 Cor. 15). We must be aware, however, of the *contextual* nature of Paul's arguments and of the *variety* of his argumentative moves, as these are designed for specific contingencies.

E. The validity of locating Paul's coherent center on a subtextual level depends on its proximity or distance to the text of the letters, that is, on the transparency of the coherent center in the text.

F. The claim of the text and its appropriation by Christians today cannot be asserted without the presence of a coherent center in Paul's thought, because it marks the abiding truth of his gospel.

G. Paul's hermeneutic challenges every interpreter of the gospel to a similar task, to construct the relation between the center of the gospel and its necessary embodiment in contingent situations in such a way that the abiding word of the gospel can become a word on target for us.

Bibliography

Barth, Karl. *The Resurrection of the Dead.* New York: Fleming H. Revell, 1933.

Baumgarten, Jörg. *Paulus und die Apokalyptik: Die Auslegung apokalyptischer Uberlieferungen in den echten Paulusbriefen.* Neukirchen-Vluyn: Neukirchener, 1975.

Baur, F. C. *Paul, the Apostle of Jesus Christ: His Life and Work, His Epistles and His Doctrine: A Contribution to a Critical History of Primitive Christianity.* 2d ed. 2 vols. London and Edinburgh: Williams and Norgate, 1876.

Beker, J. Christiaan. *Paul's Apocalyptic Gospel.* Philadelphia: Fortress Press, 1982.

————. *Paul the Apostle: The Triumph of God in Life and Thought.* 2d ed. Philadelphia: Fortress Press, 1984.

————. "Paul's Theology: Consistent or Inconsistent?" *NTS* 34 (1988): 364–77.

————. "Paul the Theologian: Major Motifs in Pauline Theology," *Interpretation* 43 (1989): 352–65.

Belser, Johannes Evangelist. *Einleitung in das Neue Testament.* 2d ed. Freiburg im Breisgau: Herder, 1905.

Betz, Hans Dieter. "The Literary Composition and Function of Paul's Letter to the Galatians," *NTS* 21 (1975): 353–90.

Binswanger, Ludwig. "Uber Psychotherapie." In *Ausgewählte Vorträge und Aufsätze.* Vol. 1. Bern: A. G. Francke, 1947, 132–59.

137

Boers, Hendrikus. Proposal for SBL Meeting, Atlanta (1906), 1–5.

Bornkamm, Günther. *Paul.* New York: Harper & Row, 1971.

————. *Studien zu Antike und Urchristentum: Gesammelte Aufsätze.* Vols. 1–4. Munich: C. Kaiser, 1952–71.

Bruce, F. F. *Paul, Apostle of the Heart Set Free.* Exeter, Devon: Paternoster, 1977.

Buck, Charles Henry, and Greer Taylor. *Saint Paul: A Study of the Development of His Thought.* New York: Charles Scribner's Sons, 1969.

Bultmann, Rudolf. *Theology of the New Testament.* Translated by Kendrick Grobel. 2 vols. New York: Charles Scribner's Sons, 1951–55.

————. *"Elpis."* In *Theological Dictionary of the New Testament.* Edited by G. Kittel and G. Friedrich. 9 vols. Grand Rapids, Mich.: William B. Eerdmans, 1964–74. Vol. 6, 197–228.

————. *The New Testament and Mythology and Other Basic Writings.* Edited by Schubert M. Ogden. Philadelphia: Fortress Press, 1984.

Cerfaux, L. *The Spiritual Journey of Saint Paul.* Translated by John C. Guinness. New York: Sheed and Ward, 1968.

Cullmann, Oscar. *Christ and Time: The Primitive Christian Conception of Time and History.* Revised ed. Translated by Floyd V. Filson. Philadelphia: Westminster Press, 1964.

Dahl, Nils. "The Particularity of the Pauline Epistles as a Problem in the Ancient Church." In *Neotestamentica et Patristica: Eine Freundesgabe, Herrn Professor Dr. Oscar Cullmann zu seinem 60. Geburtstage überreicht.* Novum Testamentum, Supplements 6. Leiden: E. J. Brill, 1962, 261–71.

Davies, W. D. *Paul and Rabbinic Judaism: Some Rabbinic Elements in Pauline Theology.* 4th ed. Philadelphia: Fortress Press, 1980. London: SPCK, 1981.

Deissmann, Gustav Adolf. *Paul: A Study in Social and Religious History.* 2d ed. London: Hodder and Stoughton, 1926.

————. *Light from the Ancient East: The New Testament Illustrated by Recently Discovered Texts of the Graeco-Roman World.* London: Hodder and Stoughton, 1910.

Dodd, C. H. *The Meaning of Paul for Today.* New York: George H. Doran, 1920.

————. *The Apostolic Preaching and Its Developments*. 2d ed. New York: Harper & Row, 1951.

Dodds, E. R. *Pagan and Christian in an Age of Anxiety: Some Aspects of Religious Experience from Marcus Aurelius to Constantine*. Cambridge: At the University, 1965.

Drane, John William. *Paul, Libertine or Legalist?: A Study in the Theology of the Major Pauline Epistles*. London: SPCK, 1975.

Fuchs, Ernst. "Die Sprache im Neuen Testament." In *Zur Frage nach dem historischen Jesus (Gesammelte Aufsätze II)*. Tübingen: J. C. B. Mohr (Paul Siebeck), 1960, 258–79.

Hanson, Paul. "Apocalypticism." In *Interpreter's Dictionary of the Bible*. Supplementary vol. Nashville: Abingdon, 1974, 27–34.

Harnack, Adolf von. *History of Dogma*. 3d ed. 7 vols. London: Williams and Norgate, 1895–1900.

Hübner, Hans. *Law in Paul's Thought: Studies in the New Testament and Its World*. Edinburgh: T. & T. Clark, 1983.

————. "Methodologie und Theologie: Zu neuen methodischen Ansätzen in der Paulus-forschung," *Kerygma und Dogma* 33 (1987): 150–75.

Kabisch, Richard. *Die Eschatologie des Paulus in ihren Zusammenhängen mit dem Grundbegriff des Paulinismus*. Göttingen: Vandenhoeck & Ruprecht, 1893.

Käsemann, Ernst. *Perspectives on Paul*. Philadelphia: Fortress Press, 1971.

————. "The Righteousness of God in Paul." In *New Testament Questions of Today*. Philadelphia: Fortress Press, 1969, 168–82.

Keck, Leander E. "Paul and Apocalyptic Theology." *Interpretation* 38 (1984): 229–41.

Knox, John. *Chapters in a Life of Paul*. Nashville: Abingdon-Cokesbury, 1950.

Koch, Dietrich-Alex. *Die Schrift als Zeuge des Evangeliums*. Tübingen: J. C. B. Mohr (Paul Siebeck), 1986.

Koch, Klaus. *The Rediscovery of Apocalyptic: A Polemical Work on a Neglected Area of Biblical Studies and Its Damaging Effects on Theology and Philosophy*. Studies in Biblical Theology 2/22. London: SCM Press, 1972.

Kraftchick, S. J. "Creation Themes in Pauline Literature," *Ex Auditu* 3 (1987): 72–87.

Kümmel, Werner Georg. *Römer 7 und die Bekehrung des Paulus.* Untersuchungen zum Neuen Testament 17. Leipzig: J. C. Hinrichs, 1929.

Lietzmann, Hans. *An die Korinther.* 2 vols. Herdersche Kommentar zum Neuen Testament 9. Tübingen: J. C. B. Mohr (Paul Siebeck), 1949.

Lindemann, Andreas. *Paulus im ältesten Christentum.* Beiträge zur Historischen Theologie 58. Tübingen: J. C. B. Mohr (Paul Siebeck), 1979.

Lütgert, Wilhelm. *Gesetz und Geist: Untersuchung zur Vorgeschichte des Galaterbriefes.* Beiträge zur Förderung christlicher Theologie 2. Gütersloh: C. Bertelsmann, 1919.

Meeks, Wayne. *The First Urban Christians.* New Haven: Yale University Press, 1983.

Melanchthon, Philipp. "Römerbrief-Kommentar, 1532." In *Melanchthons Werke in Auswahl* 5. Edited by R. Stupperich. Gütersloh: C. Bertelsmann, 1965.

Morgan, William. *The Religion and Theology of Paul.* Edinburgh: T. & T. Clark, 1917.

Murray, Gilbert. *Five Stages of Greek Religion.* 3d ed. Boston: Beacon Press, 1951.

Nietzsche, Friedrich. "The First Christian." In *The Dawn of Day.* New York: Macmillan Co., 1903, 56–61.

Nygren, Anders. *Commentary on Romans.* Philadelphia: Fortress Press, 1972.

Osten-Sacken, Peter von der. "Gottes Treue bis zur Parusie: Formgeschichtliche Beobachtungen zu 1 Kor 1,7b-9." *Zeitschrift für die neutestamentliche Wissenschaft* 68 (1977): 176–99.

Overbeck, Franz. *Christentum und Kultur: Gedanken und Anmerkungen zur modernen Theologie.* 2d ed. Edited by Carl Albrecht Bernoulli. Darmstadt: Wissenschaftliche Buchgesellschaft, 1963.

Pascal, Blaise. "Le Mystère de Jésus." In *Pensées sur la Religion et sur quelques autres sujects.* 2d ed. Paris: Delmas, 1952, 334–37.

Patte, Daniel. *Paul's Faith and the Power of the Gospel.* Philadelphia: Fortress Press, 1983.

Petersen, Norman. *Rediscovering Paul: Philemon and the Sociology of Paul's Narrative World*. Philadelphia: Fortress Press, 1983.

Philippi, Friedrich Adolph. *Commentar über den Brief Pauli an die Römer*. 3 vols. Erlangen: Heyder & Zimmer, 1848–52.

Räisänen, Heikki. *Paul and the Law*. Tübingen: J. C. B. Mohr (Paul Siebeck), 1983.

————. *The Torah and Christ: Essays in German and English in the Problem of the Law in Early Christianity*. Finnish Exegetical Society 45. Helsinki: Finnish Exegetical Society, 1986.

Rubenstein, R. L. *My Brother Paul*. New York: Harper and Row, 1972.

Sanders, E. P. *Paul and Palestinian Judaism*. Philadelphia: Fortress Press, 1977.

————. *Paul, the Law, and the Jewish People*. Philadelphia: Fortress Press, 1983.

Schmithals, Walter. *Paul and the Gnostics*. Translated by John E. Steely. Nashville: Abingdon Press, 1972.

Schneider, Johannes. *Die Passionsmystik des Paulus: Ihr Wesen, ihr Hintergrund und ihre Nachwirkungen*. Untersuchungen zum Neuen Testament 15. Leipzig: J. C. Hinrichs, 1929.

Schnelle, Udo. "Der erste Thessalonicherbrief und die Entstehung der paulinischen Anthropologie." *NTS* 15 (1986): 207–24.

Schoeps, Hans Joachim. *Paul: The Theology of the Apostle in the Light of Jewish Religious History*. Philadelphia: Westminster Press, 1961.

Schweitzer, Albert. *The Mysticism of Paul the Apostle*. New York: H. Holt and Co., 1931.

————. *Paul and His Interpreters: A Critical History*. New York: Macmillan Co., 1951.

Stauffer, Ethelbert. *Die Theologie des Neuen Testaments*. Stuttgart: Kohlhammer, 1948.

Theissen, Gerd. "Soteriologische Symbolik in den paulinischen Schriften." *Kerygma und Dogma* 20 (1974): 282–304.

————. *Psychological Aspects of Pauline Christianity*. Translated by John P. Calvin. Philadelphia: Fortress, 1987.

Vielhauer, Phillip. "Introduction." In E. Hennecke, *New Testament Apocrypha*. Edited by W. Schneemelcher. 2 vols. Philadelphia: Westminster Press, 1963–65. Vol. 2, 581–607.

Weinel, Heinrich. *Die Wirkungen des Geistes und der Geister im nachapostolischen Zeitalter bis auf Irenäus.* Freiburg: J. C. B. Mohr (Paul Siebeck), 1899.

————. *Biblische Theologie des Neuen Testaments: Die Religion Jesu und des Urchristentums.* Tübingen: J. C. B. Mohr (Paul Siebeck), 1911.

Weiss, Johannes. *Jesus' Proclamation of the Kingdom of God.* Translated, edited, and with an introduction by R. H. Hiers and D. C. Holland. Lives of Jesus Series. Philadelphia: Fortress Press, 1971.

Wendland, H. D. *Die Mitte der paulinischen Botschaft: Die Rechtfertigungslehre des Paulus im Zusammenhang seiner Theologie.* Göttingen: Vandenhoeck & Ruprecht, 1935.

Wernle, Paul. *Die Anfänge unserer Religion,* 2nd ed. Tübingen: J. C. B. Mohr (Paul Siebeck), 1904.

Westerholm, S. *Israel's Law and the Church's Faith.* Grand Rapids: Wm. B. Eerdmans, 1988.

Whiteley, Denys Edward Hugh. *The Theology of Saint Paul.* Philadelphia: Fortress Press, 1964.

Wikenhauser, Alfred. *Pauline Mysticism.* Translated by J. Cunningham. Freiburg: Herder, 1960.

Wilder, Amos Niven. *Early Christian Rhetoric: The Language of the Gospel.* Cambridge, Mass.: Harvard University Press, 1971.

Wrede, William. *Paul.* Translated by Edward Lummis. London: Philip Green, 1910.

Index of Passages Cited

ADDITIONAL SOURCES

Index of Names